# Read What Others are Saying about Dan Poynter's Books

"Poynter is at his best when discussing such specifics as starting one's own publishing house; dealing with printers; establishing discount, credit and return policies; promoting, advertising and selling a book; and order fulfillment."
—*Publishers Weekly*

"A deeply researched how-to book on writing, printing, publishing, promotion, marketing and distribution of books."
—*The College Store Journal*

"Poynter covers the production basics but his emphasis is on the business of books."
—*Booklist*

"The strength of this book is the detailed discussion of various marketing methods."
—*Choice*

"The book is a must for those considering publishing as a business, for writers who want to investigate self-publishing, and is eminently useful for its new and old ideas to those who have already begun to do it. A fine and handy guide by a fine and successful publisher."
—*Small Press Review*

"A handy, concise and informative sourcebook.... Expertly organized and chock full of hard facts, helpful hints and pertinent illustrations.... Recommended for all libraries."
—*The Southeastern Librarian*

"All the information is here. A publisher who follows Poynter's advice can hardly go wrong."
—*The Independent Publisher*

"This is by far the best book of its kind."
—*Writing & Publishing*

"Self-publishers: This how-to book and encyclopedia will be your most important investment. Poynter points you in the right direction."
—*Teacher-Writer*

"The approach is clear and easy to use in any order and should make available answers for many writers or would-be writers with questions. Recommended."
—*Booknotes*

"Poynter is a publisher of considerable experience which he passes along in minute detail.... There is real gold here."
—*Quill & Scroll*

"The most comprehensive book I have found to date on self-publishing. This one book could save you the price of several."
—*Iowa Authors United*

---

http://ParaPub.com
800-ParaPub
**Where authors & publishers go for answers**

# Book Publishing Encyclopedia
## Tips & Resources for Authors & Publishers

Dan Poynter

Second Edition, Completely Revised

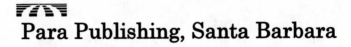

Para Publishing, Santa Barbara

# Book Publishing Encyclopedia
## Tips & Resources for Authors & Publishers

Dan Poynter

Published by:
**Para Publishing**
Post Office Box 8206
Santa Barbara, CA 93118-8206, USA
info@ParaPublishing.com; http://ParaPublishing.com

Produced in the United States of America

Soft cover         ISBN: 978-1-56860-127-4
Large print        ISBN: 978-1-56860-128-1
LIT                ISBN: 978-1-56860-129-8
PDF                ISBN: 978-1-56860-130-4
MobiPocket         ISBN: 978-1-56860-131-1
Palm               ISBN: 978-1-56860-132-8
CD in PDF, LIT, Mobipocket & Palm  ISBN: 978-1-56860-133-5

# *Contents*

These tips and resources are roughly grouped in alphabetical order. If you are reading the electronic edition (eBook), use your computer's search feature to find specific items.

Some of the URLs mentioned here will not click through. The longer URLs flow to two lines. Some email programs fail to connect them so when you click on the underlined part, the next line is not included in the address. In that case: Do not click; Copy\Paste the entire address. And check the pasted address to make sure there is not a space where the line ended.

# *About the Author*

Dan Poynter is an author of more than 120 books, has been a publisher since 1969 and is a Certified Speaking Professional (CSP).

He is an evangelist for books, an ombudsman for authors, an advocate for publishers and the godfather to thousands of successfully-published books.

His seminars have been featured on *CNN*, his books have been pictured in *The Wall Street Journal* and his story has been told in *US News & World Report*. The media come to Dan because he is the leading authority on book publishing.

His books have been translated into Spanish, Japanese, British-English, Russian and German. He has helped people to publish all over the world.

Dan shows people how to make a difference while making a living by coaching them on the writing, publishing and promoting of their book. He has turned thousands of people into successful authors. His mission is to see that people do not die with a book still inside them.

Dan was prompted to write this book because so many authors and publishers wanted to know his secret to selling so many books. Now he is revealing it to you—the good life of self-publishing.

# A Word from the Author

Here is a treasure trove of book information. I figured that since I refer to these notes constantly, perhaps other authors and publishers would find them useful too.

Many of these resources have appeared in the *Publishing Poynters* ezine. Now you can have all the tips and resources in a single, easy-to-search document.

Dan Poynter, Santa Barbara

# *Disclaimer*

This book is designed to provide information about the subject matter covered. It is sold with the understanding that the publisher and authors are not engaged in rendering legal, accounting, or other professional services. If legal or other expert assistance is required, the services of a competent professional should be sought.

It is not the purpose of this manual to reprint all the information that is otherwise available to authors and other creative people but to complement, amplify, and supplement other texts. For more information, see the many references in the Appendix.

Book writing is not a get-rich-quick scheme. Anyone who decides to write a book must expect to invest a lot of time and effort without any guarantee of success. Books do not write themselves and they do not sell by themselves. People write and promote books.

Every effort has been made to make this book as complete and as accurate as possible. However, there may be mistakes both typographical and in content. Therefore, this text should be used only as a general guide and not as the ultimate source of writing and publishing information. Furthermore, this manual contains information on writing and publishing only up to the printing date.

The purpose of this manual is to educate and entertain. The authors and Para Publishing shall have neither liability nor responsibility to any person or entity with respect to any loss or damage caused or alleged to be caused directly or indirectly by the information contained in this book.

**If you do not wish to be bound by the above, you may return this book to the publisher for a full refund.**

# A

## ADVERTISING

GREETING CARDS FOR BOOKPEOPLE are designed as bookmarks. The tall, narrow cards are perfect for writers, publishers, and booksellers. Printed on luxuriously thick textured ivory stock, with sophisticated and playful pen and ink illustrations by artist Meredith Hamilton, this one-of-a-kind greeting card makes its own distinctive mark. With 12 styles, there's one for just about everyone. In My Book® is sure to be included among your favorite cards. http://www.inmybook.com.

IMAGINATIVE IDEAS FOR YOUR SIGNATURE FILE (that file at the bottom of your email that markets you). Check out http://www.coolsig.com for ideas and quotations you can use, along with links to ASCII art (art that uses only the characters on your keyboard—so that it is not corrupted by graphics handling on the Internet). This tip from Jim Zinger

PLASTIC NAMETAG promotes business. We go to so many smaller functions where nametags are not provided. Wear your tag so people know who you are. Do not lose out on potential business. Clip-on plastic nametags run less than $4 each. Get several for your purse, attaché case, glove compartment, etc. Wear your tag at author signings so you won't be mistaken for a bookstore employee.

REFRIGERATOR MAGNETS showing your book cover. See http://www.RefrigeratorMagnets.com. (Where else?)

SCIENTIFIC ADVERTISING by Claude C. Hopkins can be read online and/or printed out free. See http://www.scientificadvertising.com. David Ogilvy said: "Nobody should be allowed to have anything to do with advertising until he has read this book seven times. It changed the course of my life."

WEAR YOUR BOOK COVER. Take your book to Kinko's. They will scan the cover and reduce it to fit on a button/badge. Wear the button to parties and other gatherings—it will get the conversations started on your favorite subject (your new book). This is very effective and very inexpensive; $3-4 each.

WHILE YOU ARE THERE, HAVE THEM MAKE A POSTER TOO. The color photocopy enlargements are usually 24" tall and laminated; they can be rolled up to fit in your luggage. Put Velcro tabs on the back for sticking to carpeted "air-walls". About $40.

## ADVICE & CONSULTATION

DAN POYNTER IS AVAILABLE TO ANSWER YOUR BOOK QUESTIONS. Call 800-PARAPUB to make an appointment. For details on consulting, see http://parapublishing.com/sites/para/speaking/edutrain.cfm

FOR A COLLECTION OF DAN POYNTER'S WISDOM on book writing, publishing, and promoting, See *Successful Nonfiction*. http://parapublishing.com/sites/para/information/writing.cfm#successful_nonfiction.

## AGENTS, LITERARY

There are an estimated 540 literary agents in the U.S.

LISTS OF LITERARY AGENTS.  See

1. Association of Authors' Representatives (AAR)
http://www.aar-online.org

2. Writers Internet Directory of Literary Agents
http://www.writers.net/agents.html
(These agents may charge a fee.)

3. http://www.authorsteam.com/agents/

4. http://www.writersservices.com/agent/index.htm

PUBLISHERS AND LITERARY AGENCIES IN NEW
YORK. Dozens of great photos and a description of the
publishing industry.
See http://clix.to/visualsofpublishing

HOW DO WE KNOW IF A MAGAZINE WILL PAY US,
AN AGENT IS HONEST, OR A PUBLISHER IS ON THE
UP AND UP? The internet makes it easier to check.
Here are some sites to look at.
http://www.sfwa.org/Beware/
http://www.anotherealm.com/prededitors/
http://www.nwu.org/ (Writer Alerts)
http://www.writersweekly.com/whispers_and_warnings.p
hp

MISERY LOVES COMPANY. Website dedicated solely to
the subject of literary rejections.
http://www.rejectioncollection.com

**AMAZON.COM**

AMAZON ADDRESS & TELEPHONE NUMBERS. The
Amazon.com Books Group is located in the international

district of downtown Seattle, WA. The mailing address for all U.S. Postal Service mail is:
PO Box 81226, Seattle, WA 98108-1226

The street address for UPS, FedEx, etc. shipments is 705 5th Avenue S. Seattle, WA 98104.

Here are the unpublished numbers we have been able to find. It appears that Amazon changes (and does not publish) numbers.

Corporate Headquarters:
(206)-622-2335
(206) 266-1000
Fax: (206)-622-2405
Seller Support: (877) 251-0696

Customer Service, U.S.
(800) 201-7575
(206) 346-2992
(206) 266-2992
(206) 266-2335
Fax: (206) 266-2950

Customer Service, Canada
(877) 586-323
Email contacts:
advantage@amazon.com
orders@amazon.com
resolution@amazon.com
charge-inquiries@amazon.com
stop-spoofing@amazon.com
reports@amazon.com
community-help@amazon.com (to report a malicious review).

REVIEWERS AT AMAZON. Check the reviews of books similar to your book at the online stores such as Amazon.com. In many cases, you can click through to the reviewer's page and find his or her email address. Email each one asking if he or she would like a copy of your book to review. These are people who are interested in your subject and want to review your book as it increases their standing with the online stores.

AMAZON.COM SALES RANKINGS. If your book is jumping between 2,000 and 9,000, you are probably selling 2-3 books per day. Here are the weekly ranges and sales:

| Rank Range | Average Sales/Week |
|---|---|
| 10,000-up | 5 or less |
| 3,000-9,000 | 15 |
| 750-3,000 | 40 |
| 450-750 | 90 |
| 200-300 | 175 |
| 100-200 | 235 |
| 75-100 | 265 |

Also see
http://www.fonerbooks.com/surfing.htm
http://www.aaronshep.com/salesranks/index.html

TRACK YOUR BOOK'S HISTORY AT AMAZON.COM. See
http://www.junglescan.com/

MULTICHECKER FOR AMAZON SALES RANKS. See
http://aaronshep.com/salesranks/index.html

BOOKSURGE SYSTEM UNDER AMAZON. The online bookseller reduces shipping costs, speeds delivery and avoids Customs by producing the books locally. In the past few months, BookSurge has grown from six to 10 plants internationally; locations now include England, The Netherlands, Spain, Poland, Greece, Australia, Panama, Mexico, the U.S., and Canada.

When a publisher or author puts a book into the BookSurge system, it automatically becomes available globally through both wholesale and retail sales channels. The retail sales channels currently include Amazon.com, Amazon.ca, and Amazon.uk, BookSurge.com, BookSurge.co.uk, as well as the two largest used bookstores Alibris.com, and ABEbooks. —Bill Green, bill.green@booksurge.com

CHANGES TO TITLES AT AMAZON. Many publishers express their frustration with the inability to contact a human being at Amazon.com for content corrections or changes. You can easily submit changes to your titles listed on Amazon.com through the "Suggestion Box" at the bottom of the page for every book. Through the online catalog update form link on the same page, you can submit changes to title, author, languages, binding, number of pages, pub date, and format/edition. Expect these changes to take 5-7 business days, and if you don't see the change by then, submit it again.

CHECK PRICES AT AMAZON WITH A CELL PHONE. According to the Economist magazine "The Japanese arm of Amazon, an online retailer, offers a service that allows subscribers to carry out a cheeky price check while browsing a bookstore. Snap a picture of the bar-code on a book or CD, and a quick over-the-air look-up will tell you if Amazon's price is lower." —Bill Frank, wafj@pacbell.net

eBOOKS AT AMAZON. For information on producing and selling eBooks at Amazon, see Document 615 at http://parapub.com/sites/para/resources/allproducts.cfm

GET YOUR COVER IMAGE ON AMAZON.COM FASTER. If you send your cover for scanning or if you send the image file on a disk, it will take weeks to post the image of your book cover. If you FTP it, the image is often posted overnight.

To FTP, you may get software such as CuteFTP or go through AOL. Here are the AOL instructions:
1. Log on.
2. In the open bar at the top, type FTP and click on "Go."
3. Click on "Go to FTP."
4. Click on "Other Site."
5. In the Site Address bar, type "FTP-1.Amazon.com." Check Ask.
6. For Login Name and Password, Click Connect.
In the "Please Enter Your Login Name" bar, type "catalog." In the "Please Enter Your Password bar," type "N3ikmJ4r."
7. Click Continue. That should get you in. You will see a lot of other JPG files that other people have uploaded.
8. Click on upload and enter a JPG, 72 dpi image file directory and name. Note that Amazon wants your cover to be identified by its ISBN. See http://www.amazon.com/exec/obidos/subst/partners/publis hers/catalog-guide.html.

LARGE PRINT BOOKS AVAILABLE AT AMAZON. Some of our books are also available in large print editions. Larger print is designed for the visually impaired, people with reading disabilities and people learning English as a second language. See these sites: http://www.amazon.com/exec/obidos/tg/detail/- /1568600887; http://www.amazon.com/exec/obidos/tg/detail/- /1568601107/. For information on how you can turn your book into large print editions and get them up on

Amazon, see Document 642 at
http://parapub.com/sites/para/resources/allproducts.cfm

**OUTSMARTING AMAZON'S INVENTORY.** Is your book listed as "On Order," with 1-2 weeks shipping, when you know they have book in their warehouse? Try selling through the "have one to sell" button on your book's page. You can list your book as a "Collectible" (such as autographed) or "Used." Collectibles have to be listed at a price greater than Amazon's selling price. Used books have to be listed at 20% less than retail. This way, your book is available "immediately" if not from Amazon.
—Cathy Stucker, http://www.IdeaLady.com.

**PUBLISHERS' PAGE AT AMAZON.COM** is at http://www.amazon.com/exec/obidos/subst/publishers.htm l. See the bar on the left for information on submitting your promotional copy and cover art.

**RETRIEVE HISTORIC AND CURRENT SALES RANKINGS FROM AMAZON** and create printable reports with 7-, 30-, 90-day and lifetime averages. See how topics or titles perform over time; measure the competition; understand what's hot. Improve decision-making; know what to publish and when. See http://www.titlez.com/welcome.aspx.

**SELLING THROUGH AMAZON.COM.** Maybe 20% of the books we sell through Amazon.com are autographed and sold through their Buy and Sell Used Items area. We sell them three ways:

1. As a signed collectible at a higher price
2. "Brand new, publisher direct, signed by author" at a slightly lower price than the new book scalpers who work Amazon.com and Halfprice.com (and then ship direct through a wholesaler)

3. Damaged wholesaler returns with autographs at a bargain rate
--Dianna Seay, Seay Communications Group & Howling at the Moon Press. DC51445@AOL.COM.)

FIVE WAYS TO MAKE AMAZON WORK FOR YOU.
--Shel Horowitz, shel@frugalfun.com.

AMAZON and B&N RANKINGS. Measuring prices and price competition online. See
http://gsbwww.uchicago.edu/fac/austan.goolsbee/research/amzn.pdf

## ANSWERING MACHINES

SECURITY TIP FROM DON PAUL. Your answering machine message should say, "I am always here, but working on my computer so I can't pick up just now." For more security tips, see:
http://www.survival-books.com/FreeHotTips.htm

TURN VOICE MAIL/ANSWERING MACHINES TO YOUR ADVANTAGE. When making follow-up calls to the media, be ready for the machine. Do not just ask for a call back—you won't get one. Instead, use a script to give a quick, complete pitch for your book/subject.
--Kate Bandos of KSB Promotions.

YOUR ANSWERING MACHINE works for you taking orders after office hours. In our 24-hour world, people expect to be able to call and leave an order in the middle of the night.

## ANTHOLOGIES

Free anthologies, e-books, and reference. See 20anthologies of articles and essays in psychology,

economics, international affairs, philosophy, and other topics. View new cyclopedias of economics and philosophy and an eBook of short fiction.
http://samvak.tripod.com/freebooks.html

## ASSOCIATIONS

WHAT CAN THE PUBLISHERS MARKETING ASSOCIATION DO FOR YOU? See
http://www.pma-online.org/memben.cfm
http://www.pma-online.org/membonly.cfm

## AUDIO BOOKS

CRITERIA LISTENERS USE IN SELECTING AUDIO BOOKS are: (1) the subject matter, (2) the author's reputation and (3) the reputation of the title, according to the Audio Publishers Association. Just as in books, buyers do not care who the publisher is.

GOODBYE AUDIO TAPES. The cassette tape is history. Detroit is changing course. We will still have audio but the tape is out...

The automakers made a mistake: They only see you once every five years. And, since 22% of the U.S. population moves each year, when you need a new car, they do not know where you are. The automakers have to find you and win you back again.

The Big Three are envious of the AOL model: getting you for a monthly subscription. The carmakers want to supply you with your music service, your roadside service, and your cell phone service. Very soon, you will get your recorded music and spoken-word audio via satellite or through your cell phone system. For more information and satellite radio service, see http://www.XMradio.com.

Record your interviews and presentations digitally and sell them as downloads. To stimulate your imagination, see http://www.Audible.com for more than 12,000 titles and 20,000 hours of downloadable audio.

For more information, see *Words on Tape* and the *AudioFile Reference Guide* by Judy Byers. Judy shares her years of experience and shows you how to design, record, duplicate, package, and sell your words. Turn your books into profitable audio downloads and CDs. To find out more and order products, see http://www.audiocp.com.

INFINITY OFFERS AUDIO-ON-DEMAND (AOD). Audio Books for the Self-published Author. Introducing the first audio book recording, CD duplication, packaging, publishing and distribution service for self-published authors. Spoken Books Publishing is accepting submissions for inclusion in their audio book publishing program. If your book is accepted, you can choose from dozens of narrators to find the person whose voice you feel is best suited for your book. Their studios are staffed by many of the best recording engineers, producers and directors in the industry. Visit www.spokenbookspublishing.com for a complete explanation of how the program works including audio samples, pricing and submission guidelines.

RESOURCE DOCUMENT. Turning Books & Speeches Into Spoken-Word Tape & Disc Products shows you the quick and easy way to turn your material into a new product. Background, tips, ideas, and resources. Document 635, 6 pages. See http://parapub.com/sites/para/information/writing.cfm and scroll down.

STATISTICS. 72.6% of spoken-word audio customers listen in their cars and 59.6% in their homes. 64.8% listen while doing other things to save time. 60% are women. The most popular categories are general fiction (entertainment) and self-help psychology. For more information, see page 3 of the Document 635, Audiotapes and Words on Tape.

NEED SOMEONE TO DESIGN AN AUDIO OR VIDEO PACKAGE? See the Supplier List at http://parapub.com/sites/para/resources/supplier.cfm

## AUTHORS

AS AN AUTHOR, publisher, or promoter, you are an information provider. Nonfiction authors provide information and you should provide your information in any form your reader wants: books, special reports, audio, video, speeches, seminars, consulting, etc. Some of your customers want your guidance (information) but are too busy to read your book. Some may commute a long distance and want your help on audio. They have time to listen to you. You are selling your expertise and research—it is called information.

AUTHORS@YOUR LIBRARY is a searchable online database that connects libraries around the country with authors and publicists looking to promote their books. See http://www.ala.org/publicprograms/authors@yourlibrary. —Ellen Metter, Browser Press.

AUTHOR v WRITER. If turning your speeches into books is a challenge, hire a ghost. You don't really believe Lee Iacocca wrote those two bestsellers all by himself do you? Lee Iacocca is the *author* but he is not the *writer.* Most celebrities do not have time to write books. —Dan Poynter, CSP, *The Self-Publishing Manual,* http://ParaPub.com.

## AUTHORS' EPIPHANIES

"If you had to identify, in one word, the reason why the human race has not achieved its full potential," observed Dave Barry, "that word would be...'meetings.'"

If I had to identify, in one word, the reason why many writers have not achieved their full potential, that word would be...email. It's so very tempting to log on in the morning when we sit down to start work. The next thing we know, it's 11:00 a.m., our energy's gone, the creative flow's disappeared, and we haven't made any progress on our book.

From now on, try checking email in the afternoon AFTER you write. You can still have a same-day response to clients—however, you'll be capitalizing on the freshness you feel in the morning and producing quality pages every day. I've found it's one of the most direct ways to turn writing frustration into effectiveness.
—Sam Horn, http://www.SamHorn.com

Note: The reflections and histories of men and women throughout the world are contained in books. America's greatness is not only recorded in books, it is also dependent upon each and every citizen being able to utilize public libraries.
—Terence Cooke

## AUTOGRAPHS, SIGNINGS, EXHIBITS

"AUTOGRAPHED BY AUTHOR" STICKERS. When you sign a book, you can bring attention to the autograph by placing a sticker on the cover. Bookstores usually get them from the American Booksellers Association The gold stickers also come on sheets and can be printed at your local photocopy or quick print center. http://www.bookweb.org.

AUTOGRAPHING TIPS. Take charge. Write your own announcement for the bookstore PA system and print up bookmarks with your advertising to have something to give away.

AUTOGRAPH PARTIES & SIGNING BOOKS shows you how to contact bookstores, whom to call, how to promote your signing, getting set up, and what to do when you are there. With resources, tips, and contacts. Document 639, 7 pages. See http://parapub.com/sites/para/information/promote.cfm. Scroll down.

BOOK SIGNINGS. LIST YOUR AUTOGRAPHING EVENT.
Bookzone: http://BookZonePro.com/calendar
Eventcaster: http://www.netread.com/calendar

BOOK SIGNING TIPS from Larry James. Check out his site at http://www.celebratelove.com/booksigningtips.htm.

MAKE A SIGN. At book fairs, autographings and industry exhibits, try this sign:

"Autographed Books are More Valuable.
Ask the author to sign your Book."

(It works!)

WHEN VISITING BOOKSTORES offer to autograph your books. Then ask if the books might be displayed in the window. It never hurts to ask for placement and the owners and/or staff often comply.

## AWARDS

AWARDS ATTRACT ATTENTION. Over 300 book awards are listed in *Literary Market Place*. Authors and publishers should submit to all in their category. Even when you do not win, many judges become familiar with your work and judges are *opinion molders*.

DO BOOK AWARDS SELL BOOKS? The big publishers say "no," according to *Publishers Weekly*. By the time the award is received, the book has been pulled from the stores and the publishers are promoting newer books. So what is the effect of an award? "It makes the author cost more when contracting for his or her next book," said one (large, New York) publisher. Fortunately, smaller publishers benefit from awards because they keep their books alive longer.

# B

### BAKER & TAYLOR

CORRECTING LISTINGS AT BAKER AND TAYLOR. Use datafix@btol.com to correct or update title information."

### BAR CODES

The bar code on a book identifies the ISBN, which in turn identifies the publisher, title, author, and edition (hardcover, etc.). The wholesalers, chains, and other bookstores will not accept your book or audiotape without a bar code. If your book arrives at a wholesaler without a bar code, they will sticker one on and charge you for it.

Further, since most books have bar codes, it will look odd without one, and your book will not be taken seriously.

**The barcode you want** is the "Bookland EAN/13 with add on" and it should be printed on the lower half of "cover 4" (the back cover) on hardcover and softcover books and on cover 2 (the inside of the front cover) on mass-market paperback books.

On mass-market paperbacks (usually sold in drug and grocery stores), the UPC barcode goes on the back cover. Cost of the UPC bar code starts at $750. To obtain a UPC, contact GS1 US (formerly called the Uniform Code Council), 7887 Washington Village Drive, Dayton, OH 45459; Tel: (937) 435-3870; Fax: (937) 435-7317. Ask for the "Price-point UPC with ISBN add-on." **Note**, you want the Bookland EAN bar code and probably do not need the UPC bar code.
info@uc-council.org; http://www.gs1us.org

The ISBN is printed above the bar code. You can get both the barcode and ISBN typeset at one place. Use the ISBN on invoices, catalogs, order forms, packing lists and the book itself. Use the bar code (with the ISBN) on the back cover of the book.

Order a free copy of *Machine-Readable Coding Guidelines for the U.S. Book Industry* from The Book Industry Study Group, 19 West 21st Street, Suite 905, NY, NY 10010; (646) 336-7141; Fax: (646) 336-6214. Obtain the publication from their website at
http://www.bisg.org/isbn-13/barcoding.html.

ISBN CHANGES. Beginning on January 1, 2007, ISBN agencies all over the world will assign new ISBN numbers that are 13 digits long, replacing the 10 digit numbers currently provided. After January 1, 2007, the

numbers issued by all ISBN agencies will have the new 13-digit structure; but as blocks of ISBN-13s built on existing ISBN-10s are exhausted, new blocks will be prefixed with 979 instead of the current 978. See
http://www.isbn-13.info/index.html
http://www.bisg.org/docs/BISG_Special_Session_09-23-04.pdf
http://www.cgpp.com/bookland/isbn.html

NEED A BAR CODE? See the Supplier List at http://parapub.com/sites/para/resources/supplier.cfm

BAR CODE PROGRAM. Free download from http://www.cgpp.com/bookland/isbn.html.

BAR CODE SOFTWARE. Get software capable of producing Bookland EAN bar codes with the price extension. See http://www.taltech.com.

GET YOUR BAR CODES IN EPS FORMAT. The specifications for barcodes are quite strict. Avoid JPEG files, since they use a "lossy" compression method and are very likely to be unreadable by the scanners.
--Pete Masterson, info@aeonix.com. Aeonix Publishing Group

**BENEFITS, READER**

OFFER BENEFITS TO READER. Special sales buyers do not buy your books, but the benefits your books can offer. Show your prospects how the content of your books will help them improve their sales, competitive position or brand profitability.
-- Brian Jud. www.bookmarketingworks.com

## BESTSELLER LISTS

A bestseller book is not like a gold record in the music industry; there is no set number that must be sold. The books' sales are compared with each other. National bestseller lists (there are several and they do not often agree) are assembled from certain bookstore and other sales reports. In addition, there are regional and specialty lists.

BESTSELLER DATABASE. More than 10 years of USA Today's weekly top 150 lists. See http://asp.usatoday.com/life/books/booksdatabase/default.aspx.

BESTSELLERS, WHAT THEY ARE AND HOW TO MAKE THEM tells you all about the various bestseller lists and how they gather their numbers. Then there is a plan for making your book a bestseller. It is packed with book promotion examples. This report is so good, it is nearly an advanced marketing plan outline. Document 612. See http://parapublishing.com/sites/para/information/promote.cfm and scroll down.

ENGLISH-LANGUAGE BOOK TOPS GERMAN BESTSELLER LIST. While Google and the major publishing houses were locking horns over Internet access to the contents of books, many of us at Frankfurt were more intrigued by the announcement that an *English-language* (Harry Potter) book topped the German best seller list, not once but *twice,* during the summer. None of us could imagine a book in French or German leading the British top ten or a Spanish-language book heading the *New York Times* Bestseller list? As a result, International Publishers Alliance had several meetings at Frankfurt on expanding and targeting its European library marketing program. If you would like more information on this program as it becomes available, please contact Godfrey Harris at hrmg@aol.com.

## BIOGRAPHIES

VIEW links to thousands of biographies, autobiographies, memoirs, diaries, letters, narratives, oral histories and more. Individual lives of the famous, the infamous, and the not so famous. Group biographies about people who share a common profession, historical era or geography. Also general collections, resources on biographical criticism and special collections. See http://www.amillionlives.com.
--Wally Bock at http://www.Bockinfo.com.

## BISAC

BISAC SUBJECT HEADINGS LIST AVAILABLE ONLINE. The BISAC Subject Headings List is a standard used by many companies throughout the supply chain to categorize books based on topical content.

The Subject Codes applied to a book can then determine where the work is shelved in a brick and mortar store or the genres under which it can be searched for in an internal database.
See http://bisg.org/standards/bisac_subject. In addition, visit a bookstore to make sure you are selecting the right category for the back cover of your book. Check the signage over the shelves where you want your book displayed.

YOUR BOOK MUST HAVE A BISAC CATEGORY listed in the upper left-hand corner or you run the risk of having it shelved in the wrong area in the bookstore. For a list of the 46 basic categories, see http://www.bookzonepro.com/insights/articles/article-40.html.

## BLOGS

BLOGGING and the Small Press. See http://www.forewordmagazine.com/ftw/ftwarchives.aspx?id=20051005.htm

BLOGGING encourages ordinary people to speak up. They're tremendous tools of freedom of expression. The Reporters Without Borders website has a handbook that explains how to set up and make the most of a blog, how to publicize it (getting it picked up efficiently by search-engines), and to establish its credibility through observing basic ethical and journalistic principles. See http://www.rsf.org/rubrique.php3?id_rubrique=542 — Charles Taormina

BLOGGING YOUR NOVEL. See http://help.blogger.com/bin/answer.py?answer=1064&topic=44

BLOGS, BLOGGING, AND BLOGGERS. All authors and speakers should have a blog: They are free to create and as a writer this medium provides an incredible way to get your thoughts in front of the world. To find out more about blogging, see http://bloggingaboutblogs.blogspot.com.

BLOGS FOR AUTHORS AND PUBLISHERS. See

http://openhorizons.blogspot.com/
http://amarketingexpert.com/2005/07/dear-reader-sharing-good-books-five.html
http://www.writers-edge.info/2005/07/writing-pointers.htm

## BOOK CLUBS

BOOK CLUBS. Many authors ask about breaking in to Book-of-the-Month Clubs like the Doubleday Book Club and the Literary Guild. It can be a challenge to turn a profit with the deep discounts commanded, but they do offer invaluable exposure and credibility. They will not return the books since they are buying the right to publish the book. If you have adequate inventory, they may purchase the product from you rather than print themselves; and if you strike a deal early enough in the game, you may be able to use this added quantity to bring down your total print costs. Many of these clubs are under the Bookspan umbrella. More information and to read the submission guidelines see www.bookspan.com.

BOOK CLUB RIGHTS. Book clubs offer you some money and a great deal of prestige. Since they were established in the mid-20s, the Book-of-the-Month-Club (BOMC) and the Literary Guild (each with over a million members) have been helping their members by selecting the best books of the thousands available at lower than normal prices. Now there are more than 200 book clubs moving over $500 million worth of books each year, most of which cater to highly specialized groups.

FOR LISTS OF BOOK CLUBS, See Literary Market Place and
http://www.book-clubs.com
http://www.book-clubs.net
http://www.bookclubdeals.com

For more information on selling to book clubs, see our Special Report *Book Marketing* at
http://parapublishing.com/sites/para/information/promote
.cfm and scroll down.

READING GROUPS (or Book Groups). Possibly the most powerful and influential marketing tool around, reading groups range from casual get-togethers in a member's home to virtual reading groups via internet chat rooms. Whatever the venue, the readers are avid and hungry for new titles to read and discuss. Many publishers have established their own reading group source websites highlighting featured selections and offering excerpts, author interviews, and suggested discussion points.

Check out www.bookmovement.com, a site devoted to fostering the growth of book clubs.

—Clint Greenleaf, CEO of Greenleaf Book Group, LP www.greenleafbookgroup.com

## BOOK FAIRS

BOOK EXPO AMERICA (BEA) DATES AND VENUES. The BEA book fair will be in:

May 18-21, 2006, Washington, D.C.
May 31-June 3, 2007, New York City
May 29-June 1, 2008, Los Angeles

Mark your calendar now.

CREATE YOUR OWN BOOK FAIR TO SELL MORE BOOKS. Contact your county public library and work with them to plan and host a Local Author Event/Expo Day. Invite all local authors. Each author should hold a reading, mini-seminar, workshop, autograph party, etc. The public library can purchase (your) books from the publisher and resell them; this way, the library will earn money. What's more, invite the local media—they love to cover community service-type events like these. And if you chair the event, you'll get double the publicity and profits.

--Eric Gelb, author of *Book Promotion Made Easy*. See http://parapublishing.com/sites/para/information/promote .cfm and scroll down.

EXHIBITING SERVICE. Association Book Exhibit, 8727-A Cooper Road, Alexandria, VA 22309;
Tel: (703) 619-5030, Fax: (703) 619-5035.
info@bookexhibit.com, http://www.bookexhibit.com. A quality on-site book service exhibiting to specialized conferences.

FOR A LIST OF BOOK FAIRS, see *Literary Marketplace* at the Reference Desk of your Public Library.

INTERNATIONAL PUBLISHERS ALLIANCE has been representing small and independent publishers at the major international book fairs for the past 14 years. For more information on this cooperative organization, send an email message with your snail mail address to Godfrey Harris, Executive Director of the Alliance at hrmg@aol.com or call (800) 966-7716. Also see http://www.harrisragan.com.

PASTE RELEVANT REVIEWS to the inside cover of your books when displaying at book fairs. Use these as your book-fair display copies. Remember, a review is a high-impact endorsement.

TRADE SHOW DIRECTORY. http://www.tsnn.com.

NEED SOMEONE TO TAKE YOUR BOOK TO TRADESHOWS? See the exhibitor services on the Supplier List at http://parapub.com/sites/para/resources/supplier.cfm


**BOOKKEEPING & ACCOUNTING**

Pub-123 PUBLISHER'S ACCOUNTING PROGRAM. Take a test drive with a free CD. Contact Alan Canton at http://www.adams-blake.com.

## BOOK SHEPHERDS

BOOK SHEPHERDS are a particular kind of consultant. They specialize in taking a book project through all the necessary steps that may include editing, design, typesetting, locating the right printer, getting a distributor, marketing and promotion (including your Web presence). Shepherds work with the author/publisher to assure that the book is produced and marketed efficiently and economically. These godparents use their experience and contacts to make sure all the publishing bases are covered and that they are covered in the right order.

Some of the better-known Book Shepherds are:

Cynthia Frank Cynthia@CypressHouse.com
Alan Gadney OneBookPro@aol.com
Barbara Florio Graham (Canada) simon@storm.ca
Brian Jud iMarketBooks@aol.com
Gail Kearns/Penny Paine Gmkea@aol.com
Greg Godek GregGodek@aol.com
Janice Phelps jmp@janicephelps.com
Linda Radke info@FiveStarSupport.com
Ellen Reid ellen@smarketing.com
Simon Warwick-Smith sws@vom.com
Ernie Weckbaugh CasaG@wgn.net
Serena Williamson Andrew, Ph.D (Canada). sw@serenawilliamson.com
Barbara Kimmel nexdec@earthlink.net
Shum F.P. (Malaysia) shumfp@pd.jaring.my
Sylvia Hemmerly PubProf@TampaBay.rr.com

The Book Shepherd: A virtual production & marketing director who is your mentor, tutor, coach and friend in the book business.
Contact them to see what each one can do for you.

## BOOKSTORES

CHRISTIAN BOOKSTORES. Many Christian bookstores order from a specific title list of books through Spring Arbor Distributors, a division of Ingram, that have been CBA (Christian Booksellers Association) flagged. The aim of Spring Arbor is to enhance people's relationship with God and spread Jesus Christ's message to the world. If your title fits the bill, talk to your distributor about submitting your book to be CBA flagged. They will need the title, ISBN, and a synopsis of the book. If the Christian connection is not clear, they may ask you to send a copy for review.
—Clint Greenleaf, CEO of Greenleaf Book Group, LLP, www.greenleafbookgroup.com

EACH TIME YOU VISIT A BOOKSTORE, find your book on the shelf and then introduce yourself to the booksellers. Tell them about your book, why it is different, and why their customers need it. Bookshop personnel are on the front lines with books and customers; they are there to help sell it.
—Susan Moss of Art Source.

INDEPENDENT BOOKSTORES. NewPages.com, an in-depth directory lists primarily general interest bookstores selling new books and periodicals. It also includes stores with more specialized subject areas: progressive bookstores, feminist bookstores, gay and lesbian bookstores, and literary bookstores.
http://www.newpages.com/bookstores

INDEPENDENT BOOKSTORES RANK HIGH IN CUSTOMER SATISFACTION. See January 2002 issue of *Consumer Reports*.
http://www.bookweb.org/home/news/btw/5310.html

INDEPENDENT BOOKSTORES DO 24% OF THEIR ANNUAL BUSINESS in November and December, according to the American Booksellers Association. The worst month is February, with 7%.

MISFITBOOKS.COM is an online bookstore that features new, rare, second-hand books, and more. See
http://www.MisfitBooks.com.

PLASTIC BOOK STANDS. We find our sales increase significantly if we give a Plexiglas counter stand to a store when we first sell them books. Most of them use the stands to display the books right at the checkout counter. This works particularly well with non-bookstores such as bike shops, gas stations, coffee shops, gift shops, etc. View and order stands at
http://www.footprintpress.com/stand.htm.
—Sue Freeman

BOOKSTORES ARE A LOUSY PLACE TO SELL
BOOKS. Go into a bookstore and look around. How many people came in to buy a book on skydiving? Now visit a parachute store. How many are interested in a book on skydiving? There are many places to sell books besides bookstore. They are easier to reach, much more lucrative and a lot more fun. To start
Thinking Outside of the Book (trade), See
http://parapub.com/sites/para/information/promote.cfm

> After taking your advice and deciding to sell my books in police uniform stores instead of the traditional book store, I just received acceptance by Borders Books and

they plan on placing a nice size order for their stores. It was the numbers that I showed them concerning the book sales in these other stores that did it. Thanks so much Rich Solita.

TO LIST YOUR BOOKS WITH THREE MAJOR ONLINE BOOKSTORES, go to:
http://www.amazon.com/exec/obidos/subst/publishers.html/104-4109396-1420718

http://www.barnesandnoble.com/help/b_faq.asp?userid=2UK6SBIQ8X&mscssid=4VEXPAB251S92J0S001PQUW69QU67D38&srefer

WHEN YOU SEE A FRIEND'S BOOK IN A BOOKSTORE, push the other books aside and turn it face out. This is just one way authors and publishers help each other.

## BRANDING

BRANDING PARTS OF YOUR BOOK AND TABLE OF CONTENTS. Branding your book sets yours apart from all the others. Notice famous authors such as Trump, who uses his name in each title. You can brand parts of your book such as your chapter titles, headings within the chapter, tips, facts or quotations.
--Judy Cullins, http://www.bookcoaching.com

## BROCHURES

COLOR BROCHURE PRINT COST CALCULATOR. Compare costs of brochure production with an ink jet printer, laser printer, copy shop, and job printer.
http://www.hp.com/sbso/productivity/color/print_cost_calc.html

NEED A BROCHURE/CATALOG SHEET PRINTER?
See the Supplier List at
http://parapub.com/sites/para/information/promote.cfm

## BUSINESS CARDS, POSTCARDS

COLOR BUSINESS CARDS AND POSTCARDS. See:
http://www.americasprinter.com
http://www.modernpostcards.com
http://www.mwmdexter.com

FOUR-COLOR BUSINESS CARDS. Many of you have admired our double-sized, fold-over business cards and requested the source. We get them from MWM Dexter, Inc. 107 Washington Ave., Aurora, MO 65605; Tel: (800) 354-9007 or (417) 887-6299; Fax: (417) 887-1822. http://www.mwmdexter.com. They do a great job on business cards, postcards, and many other specialty products. The artwork was by Robert Howard. See http://www.BookGraphics.com

POSTCARDS, BROCHURES, POSTERS, and other ad materials. See http://www.1800postcards.com.

PROMOTE YOUR WEBSITE OR BOOKS WITH LOW-COST POSTCARDS. The least expensive way to alert potential customers about your new book is with targeted email. But, if you do not have the email addresses, you may reach them with postal mail. You can't beat postcards. A postcard can have a full-color photo of your book and a sales message, and the card may be as large as 4.25 x 6 inches. Get a report from Markus Allen. He tells you where to get the best deal on postcard printing, how to qualify for postage discounts, what to put on the cards and much more. Get the report at http://www.markusallen.com/freepostcardreport.lasso?A=1428

# C

## CANADA

*CANADIAN BOOK PUBLISHING* is a north-of-the-border supplement to The Self-*Publishing Manual.* It contains all the names, numbers and resources for ISBN, copyright, Legal Deposit, CIP, bar coding, distributors, associations, magazines and much more to publish successfully in Canada. Document 628, 9 pages. See http://parapub.com/sites/para/information/business.cfm and scroll down

And *Selling Books in the US*, where one-third of the world's books are sold, Document 634 at http://parapub.com/sites/para/resources/allproducts.cfm And Suzanne Anderson's book, Self-Publishing in Canada at http://www.selfpublishing.ca/

CANADIAN DATABASE. Barbara Florio Graham keeps her Canadian libraries database up to date by asking everyone who purchases it to let her know if they have any returns. Most are happy to comply because the cost of the database, which contains more than 90 Canadian libraries with purchasing power, only costs $25 and can be used over and over again. Details at www.SimonTeakettle.com, under Resources.

## CARTOONS

ACCESS CARTOONS. Here's a wonderful site that connects you to a huge list of great cartoonists and their work.

http://epore.mit.edu/~tgowrish/tgowrish/humor/cartoon_c omic.html.

FOR CUSTOM CARTOONS FOR YOUR BOOK. Contact Andrew          Grossman,          Cartoon          Resource, andrew@cartoonresource.com, http://www.cartoonresource.com

LOVE THE NEW YORKER CARTOONS ON BOOKS? Send one to a writer or publisher colleague as a cyber greeting card. http://cartoonbank.com.

TO LICENSE NEW YORKER CARTOONS FOR YOUR BOOKS or to find out how much cartoon-licensing costs, see http://www.cartoonbank.com.

UNIQUE CARTOONS can dress up your book. Or choose a hand-watercolored 11 x 17 comic strip panel for a one-of-a-kind gift for someone at home or work. These completely unique pieces of art can be sketched, edited and illustrated in full color. Check out Jim Hunt's work at http://www.jimhuntillustration.com/custom.htm

### CATALOGS, Selling to

SELLING TO CATALOGS. 7,000 catalogs are published in the U.S. and 1,00 more are available in Canada. Each year they mail 11.8-billion catalogs to recipients. Catalogs move lots of books. You can get your book into several category-specific catalogs. See Document 625 at http://parapub.com/sites/para/resources/allproducts.cfm

### CHAINS v INDEPENDENTS

SALES TAXES are not the issue. While eTailers (web merchants) have a price advantage of not collecting sales taxes for their state, local retailers have a price advantage of not charging for shipping. Shipping costs are usually much more than sales taxes. And, the local retailer can provide instant delivery. Orders from an online store take a few days to arrive. Brick & mortar would seem to have the advantage.

The major reason the chains are able to out-perform the independent bookstores is their additional profit center: advertising. They are able to rent the space in hundreds of stores; they can us window displays, end-of-the-aisle placement, shelf-talkers, etc.

## CHILDREN'S BOOKS

According to *Publishers Weekly*, children's books fall into the following categories: 27% picture books, 17% books for babies and toddlers, 20% for younger readers, 19% for middle readers, and 17% for young-adult readers. Children's books tend to have a longer life than adult books. They start off slowly and build over time.

Today, children's books are not just sold through bookstores. They are selling through discount stores, book clubs, toy stores, food and drug stores, as well as chain and independent bookstores. Discount stores, which include Kmart and Wal-Mart, have recently had the largest market share for children's book purchases. Independent bookstores, which have a very small market share, can do well if they combine their bookstore with other specific activities, such as workshops and games that involve both children and parents.

Women buy 82% of all children's books and half are bought as gifts. Nearly 40% of the books are bought by mothers.

CHILDREN'S BOOKS, Resources for Writing, Producing and Promoting Juveniles lists the help you will need to write, produce, publish and promote this unique type of book. Document 610, 8 pages. See http://parapub.com/sites/para/information/writing.cfm and scroll down.

CHILDREN'S e-PICTURE BOOK. Even if you are not an author or publisher of children's books, you will want to see how Dragon Tales Publishing has mixed illustration, text, and sound on disk. *Dream Dragon Stories: Promoting the 3-Es: Education, Entertainment & Empowerment.* Download a free preview: http://www.dragontalespublishing.com/e_books/free_previ ew.html Fmi: Dragon Tales Publishing, P.O. Box 1949, Tustin, CA 92781, Tel: (714) 730-5386, Fax: (714) 832-9487. info@dragontalespublishing.com; http://www.dragon4kids.com

FULL-COLOR CHILDREN'S BOOKS can be printed digitally in short runs. Color separations and large Hong Kong printings are part of the past. This is good news to smaller and newer publishers that would like to test a new book.

=>Catalog of books & tools for children's writers: cbi@sendfree.com

=>Exclusive e-Books for children's writers: download at http://www.write4kids.com/ebooks.html

=>For a very clever book layout guide, printed as a children's book, contact BookJustBooks.com, Ron Pramschufer, 51 East 42nd Street, Suite 1202, New York, NY 10017, Tel: (800) 621-2556; Fax: (212) 681-8002 ; http://BooksJustBooks.com; ron@rjcom.com

=>One of the best consultants for children's book is Penny Paine, award-winning author, publisher and production specialist. Tel: (805) 569-2398. PennyPaine@aol.com.

=>"Secrets of Writing for Kids" e-report for beginners: writingtips@sendfree.com

HOW TO GET STARTED AS A CHILDREN'S WRITER. A wealth of free information is available to aspiring children's writers at www.Write4Kids.com. Ask for their newsletter, *Children's Book Insider.*

CHILDREN'S BOOKS: Resources for Writing, Producing and Promoting Juveniles lists the help you will need to write, produce, publish and promote this unique type of book.
Document 610, 5 pages. See and scroll down at http://parapublishing.com/sites/para/information/promote .cfm

## COLLABORATION

CO-AUTHOR OR GHOSTWRITER. Is There a Book Inside You?, *Writing Alone or With a Collaborator* by Dan Poynter and Mindy Bingham. You will discover: How to pick your topic, how to break it down into easy-to-attack projects, how and where to do research, a process that makes writing (almost) easy, how to improve your material, how to manage writing partnerships, how to evaluate your publishing options, as well as how to develop an individualized and workable plan. They will show you how to write your book, get the help you need and publish or get it published. With self-paced quizzes and resources. A Writer's Digest Book Club main selection. Book alone: 978-1-56860-046-8. Softcover, 5.5 x 8.5, 236 pages. See
http://parapub.com/sites/para/resources/allproducts.cfm

## CONFERENCES

MAUI WRITERS CONFERENCE ON TAPE. Bestselling authors can be outstanding speakers. For a list, see http://www.vwTapes.com.

THE MAUI WRITERS CONFERENCE is scheduled for Labor Day weekend. View and/or print out the entire program http://www.mauiwriters.com.

## CONSIGNMENTS

CONSIGNMENTS ARE HANDLED WITH AN INVOICE NOT A CONTRACT. For consignment sales, please note that you do not need our very popular product, *Publishing Contracts on CD* (http://www.parapublishing.com/sites/para/information/business.cfm) Just use your invoice and write "Consignment" in the Terms box. All you need is a record of the transaction—including the terms of sale. (We receive this question regarding consignment and contracts quite often.)

## CONSULTANTS, BOOK PUBLISHING

NEED A CONSULTANT ON BOOK PUBLISHING AND PROMOTING? See the Supplier List at http://parapub.com/sites/para/resources/supplier.cfm

CONSULTING. Dan Poynter is available for one-on-one private consulting. He can help you in Santa Barbara, at your place or over the telephone. Most consulting is by telephone. See http://parapublishing.com/sites/para/information/access.cfm?report=137&refpage=edutrain.html

HELP FOR SMALL BUSINESSES, HOME BUSINESSES, SELF-EMPLOYMENT and careers. —Janet Attard. http://www.businessknowhow.com/

FOR BUSINESS HELP. See http://www.smallbusiness.com/

RUNNING YOUR BUSINESS. http://parapub.com/sites/para/information/business.cfm

WHAT IS YOUR PUBLISHING COMPANY WORTH? See http://www.bizmark.net/Articles/article31.htm and http://www.ivanhoffman.com/selling.html

Also see BOOK SHEPHERDS

## COOKBOOKS

COOK BOOKS. Resources for writing, producing and promoting this unique type of book. Document 613, 7 pages. See http://parapub.com/sites/para/information/writing.cfm and scroll down.

COOK BOOK AUTHORS & PUBLISHERS. Paul Krupin has identified over a thousand food editors. He will fax your news release to them very inexpensively. Direct Contact Media, Tel: (800) 457-8746; Fax: (509) 545-2707; http://www.imediafax.com

COOK BOOKS, Resources for Writing, Producing and Promoting Books on Food lists the help you will need to write, produce, publish, and promote this unique type of book. Document 613, 6 pages. Scroll down. http://parapublishing.com/sites/para/information/promote.cfm

COOK BOOKS: Resources for Writing, Producing and Promoting Books on Food lists the help you will need to write, produce, publish and promote this unique type of book. Document 613, 7 pages. See and scroll down at http://parapublishing.com/sites/para/information/promote .cfm

## COMPANY NAMING

CHOOSING A NAME FOR YOUR PUBLISHING COMPANY. Consider these eight factors:

* Alphabetical placement
* Cleverness (can be positive or negative, depending on the biz)
* Descriptiveness
* DotCom and 800 number availability
* Expandability
* Personal vs corporate
* Tone
* Trademark-ability; name protection.

From *Grassroots Marketing: Getting Noticed in a Noisy World* by Shel Horowitz.

## COMPUTERS & SOFTWARE

LAPTOP ADVICE: Limit traveling with your notebook computer. Sooner or later, it will be stolen. They are too easy to steal and too valuable to pass up.

MOUSE SHOULDER. If your arm hurts after many hours at your computer, the pain may be due to your trackball. Many trackballs require the thumb to click vertically. This is an unnatural movement for your thumb. Go back to a traditional mouse or get a trackball where the thumb clicks horizontally. We like the Microsoft IntelliMouse TrackBall. Your arm will thank you.

THE CLICK-AND-SNIFF COMPUTERS ARE COMING. Soon you will be seeing smell-sensing technology in advertising, shopping, travel, and game settings.

TO UPGRADE A LOT OF YOUR WINDOWS® SOFTWARE FOR FREE, log on to http://www.microsoft.com/ie/ie40/download/rtw/x86/en/download/addon95.htm

FAST, NO-COST, SHORT-TERM ONLINE STORAGE. Ever need to get a large computer file to someone but it's too big to email or you have to get it to several people in a short period of time? Then check out http://www.sendmefile.com/howto.htm (link is to their How To page as their home page is a little busy with the ads that support the site). This service is no-cost, no registration required. You can upload a file of up to 100 Mb in size and keep it stored on their servers for 28 days. You can upload files at their site or download either their IE or Firefox compatible toolbars for uploading files directly from your browser.
--JimZinger@JimZinger.com

## CONSULTANTS, BOOK

Cypress House, Cynthia Frank, 155 Cypress Street, Suite 123, Fort Bragg, CA, 95437-5401. Tel: (707) 964-9520; (800) 773-7782; Fax: (707) 964-7531; Cynthia@cypress.com; http://www.cypresshourse.com. Editing, production and promotion services available for new publishers. Personalized and reasonable.

Penny Paine. Specializing in children's picture books. Tel: (805) 569-2398; Fax: (805) 563-0166; http://www.pennypaine.com; pennypain@aol.com.

Dan Poynter, PO Box 8206 Santa Barbara, CA 93118-8206. Tel: (805) 968-7277; Fax: (805) 968-1379. See http://ParaPublishing.com or write to Dan at DanPoynter@ParaPublishing.com. Nonfiction book promoting, marketing, and distributing. Hire Dan to speak to your group.

FREE NUTS-AND-BOLTS BOOK TIPS in a monthly eMag, "The Book Coach Says...", available from Judy Cullins at http://www.bookcoaching.com.

*TWISTING TIMES,* an ezine from MarketAbility is available free. It is full of book promotion tips and ideas. See http://www.MarketAbility.com.
Also see http://parapub.com/sites/para/resources/supplier.cfm

## COPYRIGHT, LIBRARY OF CONGRESS & LCC

COPYRIGHT may be registered before your manuscript is published, but, unless you are passing a lot of copies around for technical proofing and comment, you might just as well do as most publishers do: Wait for books to come off the press. Your work is automatically copyright *protected* under Common Law because you created it; it just isn't copyright *registered* yet.

Write to the Register of Copyrights, Library of Congress, Washington, DC 20559 and request three copies of Form TX (for registering books) and copies of Circular R1, *Copyright Basics,* and Circular R2, *Publications of the Copyright Office.* Upon receipt, read over these publications and order any others you feel you need. The

Copyright Office will also send you some business reply mailing labels so that you may send them the copyright form, your check, and the books for registration. Their telephone numbers are (202) 707-9100 (hotline) or (202) 707-3000. For forms: http://www.loc.gov/copyright/forms/.

To register your copyright, follow these three steps:
1. Print the copyright notice on the copyright page (title page verso). The notice takes the following form for example: "© 2006 by Robert Howard." You may use the word "copyright," but the "©" says the same thing and it is necessary for international protection. Also add "all rights reserved" and expand on this if you like. Check other books. The copyright notice must appear in *all* copies of the book to protect you, so double check it and all the numbers on the copyright page every time you proof copy, boards, bluelines, etc.

The copyright should be in the name of the owner. The owner may be the author, the publishing company, or whoever created or paid for the work.

2. Publish the book. Check for the copyright notice before any of the books are distributed.

3. Register your claim with the Copyright Office within three months of the book coming off the press. To do this, send a completed Form TX, two copies of the "best edition" of the book and a fee of $30. The "best edition" would be the hardcover if both the hardbound and softcover came from the printer at the same time. However, since the hardbound edition often takes longer to produce, the softcover may be the "best edition at the time of publication." If you enclose softcover copies with the Form TX, be sure to note that they were produced first.

The Copyright Office will add a registration number and date to the form and will send you a photocopy containing a seal and the Registrar's signature. The time it takes the Copyright Office to process your application varies. Nine months is not unusual. The office receives more than 600,000 applications each year.

The new copyright term is for the author's life plus seventy years. Your ownership of the book is now a valuable part of your estate, so be certain your copyrighted material is mentioned in your will.

To determine if an existing Work is still covered by copyright, see
http://www.copyright.cornell.edu/training/Hirtle_Public_Domain.htm
and
http://www.unc.edu/~unclng/public-d.htm
Also see
http://www.copyright.cornell.edu/

Copyrights protect you like a patent, but they are cheaper and much easier to secure. Like a patent, however, you must always be on the lookout for infringers. The copyright protects your text, photographs, drawings, maps, everything in the book, except the title.

**Library of Congress Preassigned Control Numbers.** The LCCN or PCN number appears on the copyright page of each book and are also included in lists and reviews appearing in the leading journals of the book trade. The PCN differs from the ISBN in that one ISBN is assigned to each different *edition* of a work (hardcover, softcover, etc.); the PCN number is assigned to the work itself, no matter how the books are printed or bound. Use of the number enables subscribers to the Library of Congress's Catalog Card Service to order bibliographic data by number and thus eliminate the searching fee. PCN numbers are essential if you want to sell to libraries. About 20,000 libraries from all over the world subscribe to this service, and some order almost every catalogued book. Additionally, most of the books are listed in *The National Union Catalogue*, issued several times a year in four editions. Most public and private libraries subscribe to it.

The PCN must be requested prior to the publication of the book so that the number may be printed on the copyright page. The Copyright Office does not preassign numbers to books that are already in print (it is too late to print the number in the book).

Catalog card numbers are preassigned only to books that the Library of Congress assumes will be added to library collections or for which they anticipate substantial demand for PCN bibliographic data. The types of material which the Library collects only in a very limited way and for which PCN numbers are generally not available include: calendars, laboratory manuals, booklets of less than 50 pages, brochures, advertisements, bank publications designed for customers, blueprints, certain kinds of light fiction, privately printed books of poems, religious materials for students in Bible schools, catechisms, instructions in devotions, individual sermons and prayers, question and answer books, most elementary and secondary school textbooks, tests except for standard examinations, teachers' manuals, correspondence school lessons, translations from English into foreign languages, picture books, comic strip and coloring books, diaries, log and appointment books, prospectuses and preliminary editions, workbooks, and vanity press publications. Since the people at the Library of Congress sometimes confuse self-publishing with vanity publishing, it is best to fill out the forms using different names for author, publisher, etc.

New publishers should contact to the Copyright Office, http://www.LOC.gov or http://www.Copyright.gov and secure "Procedures for Securing Preassigned Library of Congress Catalog Card Numbers" and their "Request for Preassignment of PCNC Number" application (Form 607-7).

http://www.loc.gov/loc/infopub/. Their telephone number is (202) 707-6372. The Forms Hotline is (202) 707-9100. The info line is 202-707-3000. or Tina Chubbs, tchu@loc.gov.

You must complete the Application to Participate and obtain an account number and password. Then you can apply for a PCN. Then the Library of Congress will send you your number. See

http://pcn.loc.gov/pcn/pcn007.html and http://ecip.loc.gov/pls/ecip/pub_signon?system=pcn

The first two digits of the PCN number do not indicate the year of publication, but the year in which the card number is preassigned. If you register after January 1, your book will appear to be a year newer. Ever wonder why the dates on films are in Roman numerals?

The PCN Office must be advised of all subsequent changes in titles, authors, etc., and cancellations. This notification is important as it prevents duplication of numbers. A new number is not necessary when changes are made. Confirmations of changes will not be acknowledged unless requested by the publisher.

There is no charge for the preassignment of a card number. An advance complimentary copy of each publication must be sent to the CIP Office, Library of Congress, Washington, DC 20540. This copy is used for final cataloging so that cards may be printed before the book is released. The CIP Office provides postage-free mailing labels for use in sending these advance publications.

COOKBOOK RECIPES AND COPYRIGHT. Mere listings of ingredients as in recipes, formulas, compounds or prescriptions are not subject to copyright protection. However, where a recipe or formula is accompanied by substantial literary expression in the form of an explanation or directions, or when there is a combination of recipes, as in a cookbook, there may be a basis for copyright protection. See http://www.copyright.gov/fls/fl122.pdf.

BOOK CATALOGING TRANSLATED. Now you will understand all the cryptic cataloging information on the copyright pages of books. http://www.ala.org/library/fact18.html

CATALOGING IN PUBLICATION is a separate Library of Congress service that supplies additional cataloguing numbers that may be printed on the copyright page of the book. These numbers help libraries to shelve your book in the correct category. Having the data block also makes the smaller and newer publisher appear to be established. During 1990 and 1996, the CIP office ran out of funds and stopped accepting new publishers into the program for several months. This may happen again.

Once you have published three books, you are eligible to participate in the CIP program and receive library-cataloguing data for printing on your copyright page. The Cataloging in Publication Office supplies postpaid mailing labels once you have been admitted to the CIP program. See http://www.loc.gov and http://cip.loc.gov.

The Copyright Office is operationally separate from the CIP Office. But the CIP and Catalog Card Number offices are the same. Catalog card numbers may be applied for per the above or when applying for Cataloguing in Publication Data.

Apply for your numbers and listings in this order: ISBN, PCIP, LC number, and then send in the ABI form.

QUALITY BOOKS PROVIDES PCIP. Quality, the library distributor, has been providing an alternative to publishers seeking CIP Data Blocks for several years (since we suggested it to them). Cataloging in Publication is provided by the Library of Congress to publishers with three or more books. For a current fee schedule, see http://www.Quality-books.com.

Contact Quality Books for an application: 1003 W. Pines Rd., Oregon, IL 61061; Tel: (800) 323-4241 or (815) 732-4450; Fax: (815) 732-4499.

CHART SHOWING WHEN U.S. WORKS PASS INTO THE PUBLIC DOMAIN. See
http://www.unc.edu/~unclng/public-d.htm
Thanks to Garrett Craig for information.

COPYRIGHT KIT. The Periodical Writers Association of Canada (PWAC) offers a free Copyright Kit on their website. Go to:
http://www.pwac.ca/pdf/copyright_kit.pdf

COPYRIGHTS/PERMISSIONS. Contact Publishing Management Consultant Jack McHugh at j.b.mchugh@worldnet.att.net. Visit his website at http://www.johnbmchugh.com.

FOR COPYRIGHT INFORMATION, see
http://www.copyrightwebsite.com
http://www.copylaw.com/

GET COPYRIGHT INFORMATION AND FORMS in PDF format so you can print them out.

http://www.copyright.gov/circs.

INTELLECTUAL PROPERTY is the branch of law which governs the ownership of ideas and their expressions. Patents are usually for mechanical devices or chemical processes. Trademarks serve to identity the source of goods in the market; copyrights protect the expression of an idea in a fixed and discernible medium.
—Rich Schell, JD, 847-404-2950,
schell@wagneruslaw.com.

LCCN ONLINE. To get a Library of Congress Catalog Card number online, see
http://pcn.loc.gov/pcn/pcn006.html or call (202) 707-9808.

THE TIME IT TAKES THE COPYRIGHT OFFICE TO PROCESS YOUR APPLICATION varies. Nine months is not unusual. The office receives more than 600,000 applications each year.

WHEN DO COPYRIGHTS EXPIRE? For a free and extremely valuable chart, see
http://www.unc.edu/~unclng/public-d.htm

IF YOUR BOOK IS COMING OFF THE PRESS JUST BEFORE THE END OF THE YEAR, put the next year's date on the copyright page. Both the book industry and consumers like "new" books. Do not send in Copyright Form TX until after the first of the year.

### CONTRACTS & AGREEMENTS, LAW & LEGAL

BOOK ATTORNEYS. Whenever you are contracting over serious money, we strongly recommend you seek legal advice. For a list of lawyers specializing in book law, see Lawyers on the Supplier List at

http://parapub.com/sites/para/resources/supplier.cfm. And
Document 113 at
http://parapub.com/sites/para/information/access.cfm?isbn
=Document%20113&qty=1&isdl=1

CONTRACTS. The person who drafts the contract has
control over the agreement. We can supply you with
Contracts on Disk (so you do not have to keyboard them),
books to explain book contracts and a list of book-
publishing attorneys. Be smart and supply your own
contract. See all the resources in this section.

FIFTEEN ITEMS TO NEGOTIATE IN YOUR NEXT
AUTHOR-PUBLISHER AGREEMENT. Compare this
checklist and tip sheet to your contract to ensure you've
not forgotten anything. Remember, contracts may vary,
but they should all contain these important provisions.
See
http://copylaw.com/forms/pubchk.html

PUBLISHING CONTRACTS ON CD, Sample
Agreements for book publishers is a collection of the 22
most-needed legal documents covering every facet of the
book publishing business including: An author-publisher
contract for a trade book, a publisher-illustrator
agreement, a foreign rights agreement and 19 more. Just
put the CD into your computer, bring the appropriate
contract to the screen, fill in the names, and check the
suggested percentages. Then print out these lengthy
contracts. You do not have to draft the agreements; you
do not even have to type them. One of our most popular
publishing tools. ISBN 978-0915516-46-9 Compact disk.

Some of our Special Reports are available on CDs to save
you all the keyboarding. Available for the PC and Mac.
See

http://parapublishing.com/sites/para/information/business
.cfm and scroll down. Call Para Publishing at 800-
ParaPub to order.

PUBLISHING CONTRACT: AUTHOR—PUBLISHER.
This is a primary Trade Publishing Agreement for use
between a publisher and an author for trade hardcover
and softcover editions. A new paragraph covers electronic
rights. Document 607, 15 pages, See
http://parapublishing.com/sites/para/information/business
.cfm. Scroll down.

### CUSTOMER or CLIENT?

HOW DO YOU REFER TO THOSE WHO SEEK YOUR
ADVICE through your books, seminars and consulting?
Jay Abraham advises they are not "customers," they are
"clients." A customer is just a buyer who has no special
relationship with you. A "client," on the other hand, is a
special person who is under your care and protection.
Since you are pursuing repeated sales, refer to your
"valued clients." Do not treat those who come to you as
(one-time) customers. See http://www.Abraham.com.

NOTE: the secret to great customer service is not
"smiling." The secret is making the customer smile.

### COVERS & JACKETS, BOOK

BOOK COVERS. When do you need to design them? See
http://www.BookCoverTips.com
—Kathi Dunn

COVERS THAT SELL BOOKS. Everyone knows you
should not judge a book by its cover but everyone does.
Your distributor, wholesalers, bookstore buyer, and
ultimate customer all make buying decisions based on the

cover; none read the book first. Your cover is your primary marketing tool. Learn the secrets of good cover design and where to get professional design help. Document 631, 12 pages. See http://parapub.com/sites/para/information/produce.cfm. Scroll down.

DO NOT LIST YOUR URL ON THE BACK COVER of your book. Bookstore browsers may delay the purchase figuring they can get free information from your website. For more information on covers, see: http://parapub.com/sites/para/information/produce.cfm and scroll down.

IS YOUR COVER WORTH $50? Did you know the average reader spends only eight seconds glancing over a book cover before making a decision to buy? Make the most of those eight seconds! Our evaluation will help you determine whether or not your book makes the eight-second cut! Experienced publicist and editor will provide a one-page evaluation of your cover, looking at design, key words and phrases, and things you need to know that will make a difference between making a sale and having your book stay on the shelf.
—Penny Sansevieri and Melanie Rigney at penny@amarketingexpert.com

CHECK OUT BOOK COVERS within and without your genre. Visit a book store or go on line to Amazon.com. Observe how type and images are used. Why are some covers more appealing than others? Adapt what you like to your own cover.
—Robert Howard, the Cover Artist.
www.bookgraphics.com

THE OUTSIDE OF YOUR BOOK SELLS THE INSIDE
—Ron "Hobie" Hobart,

http://www.BookCoverTips.com

BOOK COVER DESIGN SHEET. A paint-by-the-numbers outline to aid you in writing your back-cover sales copy. See Document 116 at http://parapub.com/sites/para/resources/allproducts.cfm

DUST JACKET COVERS - PAPER CHOICE
--- Karen Ross 310-397-3408
http://www.karenross.com

Paper... most are glossy, laminate, UV, etc., but have you really looked and felt them all...? Some are a delightful linen or uncoated stock that for, the right book, can really bring home another 'sense' to the reader. And for your paperbacks... be sure to get samples from the printer on 10 or 12 pt CS1 stock... the weight makes a difference too.

SHOW ME SOME SPINE!
--Kathi Dunn, Dunn+Associates Design,
http://www.dunn-design.com

A large number of book store patrons are strictly browsers. They know they want something to snuggle up with on the couch, on the beach or on that long flight. . . they're just waiting for something to catch their eye. In book stores, your book will probably be displayed spine-out, fighting for attention among a line of other books in the same genre. The spine is a critically compelling component usually seen before the prospective consumer even gets to that all-important front and back cover. That spine has to stand out, attract attention, and say, "Pick me up!" So, when designing your book cover, think of the spine as a miniature billboard. Add a compelling visual element and make certain the title is readable on this narrow band of real estate. Develop the interior design of the book so its page count generates a spine of a half-inch or more. This will give your book's spine greater opportunity to complete on the shelf. If your page count is over 224, you will likely make the half-inch mark. If not, ask about high-bulk paper to thicken up the book and to leverage your spine's opportunity to jump off the shelf.

TITLE AND SUBTITLE PLACEMENT. Typically a book title is placed in the top 1/3 of the cover. It should not be obscured by a busy or a low-contrasting background. If this is an issue, try placing a solid colored rectangle behind the tile.
The subtitle follows the title and can be positioned left, right or centered. Its placement is most often dictated by the image or graphic used. If necessary, it can be broken up to form more than a single line.
—Robert Howard. www.bookgraphics.com

NEED A COVER DESIGNER? See the Supplier List at http://parapub.com/sites/para/resources/supplier.cfm

# D

## DEMOGRAPHICS

DEMOGRAPHIC RESOURCE. Who is living where? Check any neighborhood. Type in a Zip Code at http://www.melissadata.com/Lookups.

## DESIGN, TYPESETTING & LAYOUT (BOOKS)

BOOK DESIGN. To get what you want, just buy one. Visit a bookstore. Check your section, then look into other sections. Find a book you like—on any subject. Consider binding, layout, feel, margins, type style, everything. Then buy it. Use this book for a model. Tell your typesetter and printer you want your manuscript to look like this book. Buy a model book.

BOOK DESIGNER LISTSERV. A place for authors, typesetters, designers, publishers, etc. to exchange ideas that will help self-publishers create professional-looking books to compete with those produced by larger publishing houses. See
http://groups.yahoo.com/group/publishingdesign/

## DESIGN, BOOK

INTERIOR BOOK DESIGN. Tip: The first paragraph in chapters looks and reads better if the indent is omitted and the line is flush left. This allows the reader a "strong" beginning point. Books can be made longer by using simple layout tweaks, such as increasing type size, leading and margins.
—Karen Ross, karen@karenross.com.

PUT AN ORDER BLANK ON THE LAST PAGE OF YOUR BOOK—facing out. Let readers know precisely how much to send for the book, shipping, and sales tax (if in the state) so they can send copies to their friends. Offer your other books or products too. Order blanks are the easiest promotion you can do for your book—and they work.

TIP: LIBRARIES DO NOT BUY FILL-IN TYPE BOOKS. They do not want their clients to write in the stock. On the other hand, fill-ins can often be changed to lists. Eliminate fill-ins if you can.

REPRODUCING CHARTS, GRAPHS & TABLES IN YOUR BOOK'S INTERIOR
··· Karen Ross 310-397-3408 http://www.karenross.com

Most manuscripts I receive have the charts, graphs and tables already made exactly the way the author wants them so sometimes redoing them can be not only costly but unsettling.

Most of the time the illustrations can be exported from MS Word exactly the way they were created and look good in reproduction. Be sure to consult with your book designer when the time comes... they can really help you with the process.

PRODUCING YOUR BOOK. Design, typesetting & printing. Electronic and audio books. http://parapub.com/sites/para/information/produce.cfm

NEED A BOOK DESIGNER/TYPESETTER? See http://parapub.com/sites/para/resources/supplier.cfm

## DESIGN, PROMOTIONAL MATERIALS

Dunn + Associates, Ron "Hobie" Hobart, P.O. Box 870, Hayward, WI 54843. Tel: (715) 634-4857; Fax: (715) 634-5617. Hard-selling, pick-me-up audio, CD, cover design. info@dunn-design.com; http://www.dunn-design.com

Robert Howard Graphic Design, Robert Howard, Tel: (970) 225-0083; rhoward@bookgraphics.com; http://www.BookGraphics.com Cover designs for books, CDs and DVDs, posters, logos, web images and more.

## DIRECT MAIL

BOB BLY'S *DIRECT RESPONSE LETTER* is full of free tips for doubling your response rates. See http://www.bly.com.

DIRECT MAIL FOR BOOK PUBLISHERS shows how you can compete with the larger publishers by taking your message directly to the reader. Study the rules of direct mail and email such as repetition, timing, response formulas, and profit analysis. Learn to find and evaluate lists. Follow the plan for drafting your brochure and cover letter; assemble a direct mail package that brings results. This Report also shows you how to assemble your own lists to rent to others—providing you with a new profit center. If you have a non-fiction book with an identifiable audience (and can find or assemble a mailing list for it), you may use direct mail and email successfully to sell books. See Doc 142. ISBN 1-56860-030-5; 38 pages. See http://parapub.com/sites/para/resources/allproducts.cfm

NEVER SEND A DIRECT-MAIL SOLICITATION WITHOUT A COVER LETTER. Your letter must "introduce" the recipient to the brochure and tell him or her why it is worth reading.

## DIRECTORIES AND DATABASES

BOOK DIRECTORIES. Register your books so that buyers can find them. See Document 112, *Poynter's Secret List of Book Promotion Contacts* (free) at http://parapub.com/sites/para/resources/allproducts.cfm. Scroll on down.

GET LISTED WITH THE SMALL BUSINESS ADMINISTRATION FREE. Submit your online business card at http://app1.sba.gov/buscard. Click on "Add a Card" and fill out the form. Thanks for this tip from Anne Grimm-Richardson, tiptoe literary service, www.willapabay.org/~anne.

LIST YOUR BOOK FREE ON THE PARA PUBLISHING WEBSITE (ParaSite?). Include bibliographic data, a

description, ordering, and email addresses and URL (orders and inquiries go directly to you). See Success Stories:
http://parapublishing.com/sites/para/resources/successstories.cfm

PROGRAMS AND SERVICES AVAILABLE. Before you start your publishing company, you should take 10 minutes to call the local small business development center in your area to find out what programs and services are available in your area to help you with state local and regulatory requirements. The best legal client is an informed one. Many small business development centers offer workshops on taxes and business entities among other topics.
—Rich Schell, JD (847) 404-2950
schell@wagneruslaw.com.

REGISTER YOUR BOOK IN THE BOOKSXYZ DATABASE FREE. See http://www.booksxyz.com.

## DISCOUNTS ON BOOKS.
Dealer Bulletin; example of the discounts offered to dealers. See Document 138 at
http://parapub.com/sites/para/resources/allproducts.cfm
and
Dealer Pricing. For those who wish to buy in quantity for resale.
http://parapub.com/sites/para/resources/resale.cfm

## DISPUTES

DISPUTE RESOLUTION PROGRAM. Members of the Publishers Marketing Association who have a trade dispute with a printer, distributor, or other supplier to the book industry may apply to the PMA for help in resolving the matter. The intent is to resolve the dispute before it becomes complicated and expensive. For more information, Contact the PMA, Tel: (310) 372-2732; http://www.pma-online.org

## DISTRIBUTORS, WHOLESALERS & DEALERS

BOOK PUBLISHERS NEED AN EXCLUSIVE DISTRIBUTOR to sell their books to the wholesalers, chain bookstores, and independent bookstores. Bookstores are computerized; they use bar codes to track books. They do not want to deal with, and write checks to, thousands of publishers each month; they would rather deal with a handful of wholesalers and distributors. Most stores order from Ingram, but as a wholesaler Ingram does not have sales reps to show your books. You need a distributor with reps. The secret is to find the right distributor for your book.

Distributors have sales reps that visit the stores, show your book (cover) and take the orders. There are more than 85 book distributors and each specializes in certain types of books. Publishers must match their line of books to the distributor in order to ensure that the distributor's sales reps are visiting the right bookstores and can talk up the book. BTW, Ingram and Baker & Taylor are wholesalers not distributors; they fill orders but do not have sales reps. For a list of distributors and their lines of specialty, see our Special Report *Book Marketing: a New Approach* and Document 605, *Locating the Right Distributor* at http://parapublishing.com/sites/para/information/promote.cfm. Scroll down.

If you still can attract the right distributor for your book, you can move to Plan B. Here are three people who can line you up with a distributor.

=>Rebecca Austin: (231) 933-4649; AandN@aol.com

=>Alan Gadney: (818) 340-6620; OneBookpro@aol.com

=>Simon Warwick-Smith: (707) 939-9212; Warwick@vom.com; http://www.warwickassociates.net.

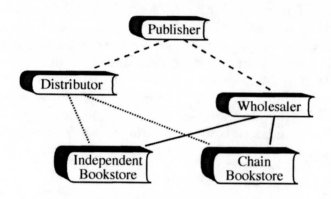

THE BOOK TRADE

DISTRIBUTORS TRIMMING LISTS. The reality of the 80/20 rule is being noticed by book distributors. Both Greenleaf Distribution and Biblio are cutting out the dead wood. According to industry observer Dan Poynter, "the fault usually lies with the author/publisher. Distributors can only get your book into the bookstores. It is up to the author publisher to promote the book to get the (buying) customers into the stores to pull the book through the system. The problem is that many publishers, upon securing a distributor, figure the stores are "covered" and they concentrate on other parts of their business."

Biblio has cut their vendor list by 17% so far and they are aiming for a 45% cut. Biblio will require marketing plans. Greenleaf took a more humane approach; they sent letters out to vendors giving them to the end of the year to bring up their sales numbers.

FOR A LIST OF THE BOOK DISTRIBUTORS RECOMMENDED BY INGRAM, see http://www.ingrambookgroup.com.

IF YOU DO NOT HAVE A DISTRIBUTOR and want to submit your book directly to Borders and WaldenBooks, call their New Vendor Acquisitions Information Line at (734) 477-1333 for recorded instructions.

THE INGRAM STOCK STATUS SYSTEM (Freddie) telephone number is (615) 213-6803. Write it down. Use it to check comparative book movements (yours and those in its genre). Just punch in the ISBN at the voice prompts. You will learn how the book is moving including Ingram's sales for last year and so far this year. These numbers are not sales totals for the books but, since Ingram moves more than half the books in the U.S., the numbers are good for comparing sales between books.

TELEPHONE NUMBERS FOR THE BOOK TRADE

Bookazine
800-221-8112
201-339-7777.

Baker & Taylor
1-800-775-1100.
Electronic: 1-800-775-0419.
DVD or music orders, 1-800-775-2600.

Ingram
Phone numbers for orders:
Ingram Book Company: 800-937-8000
Spring Arbor: 800-395-5599

Ingram Library Services: 800-937-5300
Ingram International (Canada): 800-289-0687
Ingram International (other than Canada): 615-793-5000
x27652

Customer service numbers:
Ingram Book Company: 800-937-8200
Spring Arbor: 800-395-7234
Ingram Library Services: 800-937-5300
Ingram International (Canada): 800-289-0687
Ingram International (other than Canada): 615-793-5000
x32622

Koen-Levy Book Wholesalers
856-235-4444.

NACSCORP
www.nacscorp.com

Partners Book Distributing
Customer Service: 1-800-336-3137
Toll-F.ree Orders: 1-800-336-3137

Partners/West Book Distributing
1-800-563-2385 or e-mail
orders@partners-west.com.

SALES REPRESENTATION & DISTRIBUTION
OPTIONS for Independent Publishers by Tom Woll has
been published by the Publishers Marketing Association.
The 47-page report describes your distribution options,
reveals the economics of various types of distribution and
advises on managing your sales efforts. It is free to
members and $15 to nonmembers. Send your request to
PMA at info@pma-online.org and include your shipping
address.

INFOKITS. Detailed information on book writing, production, promotion and distribution.
http://parapub.com/sites/para/resources/infokit.cfm

INGRAM SALES. Punch in an ISBN for any book and hear the rate of sales for this year and last.
Tel: 615-213-6803

WANT HELP SELLING QUANTITIES OF YOUR BOOKS to Non-Traditional Markets? See:
http://www.bookzonepro.com/insights/articles/article-139.html
Contact Tim McCormick at GreenTreePub@Earthlink.net
And Brian Jud at iMarketBooks@aol.com

DEALER PRICING. For those who wish to buy in quantity for resale.
http://parapub.com/sites/para/resources/resale.cfm

MARKETING, PROMOTING & DISTRIBUTING YOUR BOOK. Wholesalers & Distributors. Book reviews, news releases, autographings, interviews, book fairs, export & foreign rights.
http://parapub.com/sites/para/information/promote.cfm

**DOWNLOADS & UNLOCKS**
DOWNLOADABLE eBOOKS
http://www.cyberread.com/ebookinfo/treebookman.asp

UNLOCKING DEVICES/DOWNLOADS. Para Publishing has been selling unlockable documents from our site for many years. Often, in the morning when I check the order-email account, I discover that we've sold dozens of reports overnight.

The customers benefited because they received the reports instantly (on a Sunday) and did not have to pay for shipping or sales tax. Para Publishing benefited because we did not have to print, inventory, wrap, ship or place postage on the reports. We did not even have to answer the telephone and write down the order. This is truly a win-win situation made possible by the Internet. Don't you love the information business?

The details: We sell well over 50 documents as PDF files from our website. Cybercash checks the client's credit card account and deposits the money into our bank account. Then the document is unlocked and comes to the screen. The client may read the document on the screen and/or print it out. This system is not a multi-step "download," it is an automatic single step "unlock" of the document. See our website for the layout. Mary Westheimer put the system together for us.

# E

## eBOOKS

EBOOKS ARE ALL PART OF THE NEW BOOK MODEL. See
http://parapublishing.com/sites/para/resources/newbook.cf
m

## TOP eBOOK SITES

1. Elegant Solutions Software and Publishing Company:
http://esspc-ebooks.com
2. eReader: http://www.ereader.com
3. Fictionwise: http://www.fictionwise.com
4. Scorpius Digital Publishing:
http://www.scorpiusdigital.com
5. Awe-Struck eBooks: http://www.awe-struck.net

6. University of Virginia's Library:
http://etext.virginia.edu/ebooks/ebooklist.html
7. Blackmask Online: http://www.blackmask.com
8. Book Locker: http://www.BookLocker.com
9. Amazon: http://www.Amazon.com

eBOOK FULFILLMENT. If you have an eBook and a website but do not want to invest in downloading software, consider an eFullfilment service. Check BookLocker and Barnes&Nobel.com.

eBOOKS MOVE TO CELL PHONES. See
http://edition.cnn.com/2005/TECH/ptech/03/21/cell.phone.
novels.ap/index.html

EVALUATE THE SERVICES OF THE DOTCOM PUBLISHERS/SERVICE PROVIDERS: POD, PQN and eBooks. Compare the services offered by iUniverse, 1stBooks, Xlibris, and more. See the comparison chart at http://www.u-publish.com/compare.htm.

FOR MORE INFORMATION ON ePUBLISHING, see http://www.impressions.com.

SEE HOW eBOOKS ARE SOLD. The Self-Publishing Manual, Writing Nonfiction and Successful Nonfiction are available for just $7.99 in electronic download from Amazon.com and other web sites. Now you can have a fully searchable edition of these bestsellers. Visit the sites and see how eBooks are sold.
http://www.fictionwise.com/eBooks/DanPoyntereBooks.ht
m and
http://www.amazon.com/exec/obidos/search-handle-
url/index=books&field-author-
exact=Dan%20Poynter&rank=-
relevance%2C%2Bavailability%2C-daterank

SELLING eBOOKS. *The Self-Publishing Manual, Writing Nonfiction* and *Successful Nonfiction* are available for just $7.99 in electronic download from Amazon.com. Now you can have a fully searchable edition of these bestsellers. Visit the site and see how eBooks are sold. And see Document 615 at http://parapub.com/sites/para/resources/allproducts.cfm

THE EBOOKS ARE HERE. The hardware and software are here and now the content is coming. The frontlist titles being offered is exploding. See the following websites:http://www.NetLibrary.com and http://www.ereader.com.

THE MAJOR EBOOK FORMATS are Adobe Acrobat (PDF), Microsoft Reader for the Pocket PC (LIT), The Rocket and the Softbook. Make sure you order the right content for your reader.

WHAT IS AMAZON THINKING? They have been discounting some bestselling books 30% for some time. For example, the brand new edition of The Self-Publishing Manual is selling for 30% off or $13.96. The eBook edition is only $7.99. Incredible! How long can this last? http://www.amazon.com/exec/obidos/tg/detail/-/1568600887

## EDITING AND PROOFREADING

PENMARK. Karen Stedman. L.A.-based. Fiction and nonfiction book editing, ghostwriting, copywriting, news releases; book marketing. Tel: (818) 902-0278; Fax: (818) 902-0576. penmarkg@aol.com; http://www.penmarkonline.com.

QUINN'S WORD FOR WORD and Brainstorm Editorial. Robin Quinn, 10573 West Pico Blvd. #345, Los Angeles,

CA 90064. Tel: (310) 838-7098; quinnrobin@aol.com.
Copyediting, writing, proofreading, manuscript
evaluation, and ghostwriting.

GRAMMAR SITE. Need to verify your grammar,
punctuation, etc?
http://grammar.ccc.commnet.edu/grammar

GUIDE TO GRAMMAR & WRITING. See
http://grammar.ccc.commnet.edu/grammar/

NEED AN EDITOR OR PROOFREADER? See the
Supplier List at
http://parapub.com/sites/para/resources/supplier.cfm

## EDUCATION & TRAINING

More than 2,000 ENERGIZED PUBLISHERS have
graduated from our weekend workshops here in Santa
Barbara since 1984. Many publishers got so much out of
the weekend, they are returning for an update on the
industry. Four times a year, 23 people invest their money
and journey to Santa Barbara to learn more about book
marketing, promoting, and distributing. The events are
held at Dan Poynter's home offices, high on a hill
overlooking the Pacific. See the ParaCalendar in our
Publishing Poynters ezine and Document 167 on our
website:
http://parapublishing.com/sites/para/information/access.cf
m?report=167&refpage=edutrain.html

SANTA BARBARA: WHERE BOOKS ARE CREATED. At
last count, this area on the central California coast
boasted of 365 book authors. With a population of about
160,000, that probably means the Santa Barbara South
Coast has more published authors, per capita, than any
other community. Some of the better-known authors are

Sue Grafton, Barnaby Conrad, Jack Canfield, Bradford Dillman, Jane Russell, Jonathan Winters, and William Peter Blatty.

Santa Barbara = Large Numbers. We noted that Santa Barbara has over 365 book authors. Now we read the median price for a home on the south coast is over $960,000. If there is a correlation between these numbers, then some local authors are doing very well.

---

**Para Publishing:**
Changing the way books are written, produced and promoted.

---

**eMAIL**

CHECKING EMAIL. You can gain access to your email from any computer on earth with Internet access. Just go to http://www.mailstart.com. Type in your email address and password. Viola, it will retrieve your email. --(Fire) Captain Bob.

DO NOT INCLUDE ATTACHMENTS TO YOUR EMAIL if you want the information to be read. Due to the proliferation of viruses, many companies and individuals have a rule against opening unknown attachments— EVER.

DOTCONS PROLIFERATE. (Yes CON) Check with the FTC on the too-good-to-be-true offers you receive via email. Some are so subtle, which makes them very scary. http://www.ftc.gov/bcp/conline/edcams/dotcon/

EMAIL MARKETING IS EFFECTIVE. According to Tim Sutherin in *Target Marketing* magazine, permission-based email marketing can be 10 times more efficient than direct postal mail, 20 times more efficient than banner advertising on websites and costs much less to deliver. He adds that another benefit is that email can be easily personalized.

HOAXES. Before you forward email with an unbelievable story, find out if it is a hoax and urban legend, see
http://www.snopes2.com
http://www.urbanlegends.com
http://www.nonprofit.net/hoax
http://www.truthorfiction.com
http://hoaxbusters.ciac.org
http://www.trusecure.com

PUT YOUR EMAIL ADDRESS on your letterhead to get a faster response. Put it on your business card to get more people to contact you. List it in directories to encourage more business. You have many addresses: postal, telephone, fax, etc. Email is one of them.

SEND HOLIDAY CARDS VIA EMAIL—many are free.
http://www.americangreetings.com/index.pd.

WANT FASTER ACTION ON AN EMAIL MESSAGE? Send a copy (cc) to another person. Then the person addressed will know there are two (or more) people waiting for action.

WANT TO TRANSLATE AN EMAIL MESSAGE OR A WEBSITE PAGE INTO ANOTHER LANGUAGE? See http://www.freetranslation.com.

HUMOR IS FORWARDED ON THE NET more than any other message. Years ago, Joe Vitale hired humor writer Paul Seaburn who drafted a Dave Letterman-style *Top Ten Reasons to Read* CyberWriting by Joe Vitale. Vitale emailed it to 49 friends with his .sig at the end and within hours, it was forwarded across the Net. See Joe's website at http://www.mrfire.com.

## ENDORSEMENTS

BLURBS FOR YOUR BOOKS, Testimonials, endorsements, and quotations. To make your book sell, you will need powerful testimonials on the back cover (3), front cover (1) and extras can go on the first page of the book. Many news releases today start with a blurb. This Instant Report gives you a simple two-step program for getting testimonials from VIPs. Document 609, 6 pages. See http://parapub.com/sites/para/information/produce.cfm. Scroll down.

## EZINES, PUBLICATIONS

BOOKFLASH BULLETIN is a free newsletter from Bookzone. It features breaking publishing news. See http://www.bookflash.com.

GALLEYGIRL is a weekly column on publishing by Time Magazine senior reporter Andrea Sachs. See http://www.time.com. The column is an eclectic mix of serious and light information about books, authors, the publishing industry, new books, what's up and coming, interviews with authors, etc.

NAWW—The National Association of Women Writers offers a FREE ebooklet. Just subscribe to the NAWW WEEKLY, the FREE inspirational/how-to ezine for women writers. Send a request to naww@onebox.com or visit http://www.naww.org.

PUBLAW UPDATE is a free ezine from the law office of Lloyd L. Rich, an attorney practicing publishing, cyberspace, and intellectual property law. See http://www.publaw.com.

STUDIO B BUZZ is a three-times a week free ezine. In a sense, it's a clipping service of ePublications or items that are pertinent to the writing/publishing world. The items are brief, but with links to the full article. See http://www.StudioB.com.

PUBLISHING POYNTERS is Dan Poynter's successful ezine. To subscribe (free) see http://parapublishing.com/sites/para/resources/newsletter.cfm. To recommend this ezine to another writer or publisher, simply forward the entire newsletter. He or she will thank you.

# F

### FAX MACHINES

TIME TO CLEAN YOUR FAX MACHINE? If your fax is over two years old, it's probably dusty inside. Insert a document and press the copy button to see what quality others are receiving from you. If the type is not clear, wipe off the mirror and lens. Call for service or get out a screwdriver. Few people realize that transmissions can deteriorate in quality, and they don't know their transmissions are bad unless recipients complain.

### FEEDBACK/PEER REVIEW

ASK FOR FEEDBACK and make it easy. Sherry Lowry gave two copies of her book to a colleague with a large SASE at a conference. The seminar leader penciled comments in the book on the flight home and mailed it to Sherry. And she showed off the other book in her next presentation. Sherry is co-author of *Discover Your Best Self - Through the Art of Coaching.*

DISCOVER THE VALUE OF PEER REVIEW. See http://www.parapublishing.com/sites/para/information/writing.cfm.

GETTING FEEDBACK. Royce (of Royce Daugherty Publishing) includes a postage-paid reply card with every book order. Although the returns average only about 15%, readers do take the time to tell us what they like most about the book.

Best of all, they rate the book on a scale of 1 to 10. So far, we're running a solid 9.9 rating! Typical response: "I loved all of it, but especially the beginning and the ending. I cried many times when I read this book ...and can't wait to read [the author's] next book."

We post "blind" results on our site and have found that the testimonials provide a nice push to other potential customers. One note of caution ... it's imperative to ask people for prior approval to list their names, cities, and state/province before publishing or posting testimonials. As a matter of procedure, we're posting blind results only, but may include names and city/state info shortly.
—Ty Royce

## FICTION & POETRY

Fiction and Poetry are a greater challenge to sell than nonfiction.

Worldwide, nonfiction (valuable information) outsells fiction (entertainment) by $55 billion to $25 billion.

POETRY AND QUOTATIONS CAN BE SOLD when included in a form or artwork. Randy Kjerstad publishes broadsides featuring his woodblock-print artwork with inspirational and thought-provoking quotations. For examples: randy@kjerstad.com

PUBLISHING FICTION & POETRY. Fiction and poetry must be sold—just like anything else. This Report will put you in touch with the right people and products: books, tapes, reports, magazines, mailing lists, contests, marketing consultants and more. It tells you how to find a publisher. Document 606, 7 pages. See and scroll down at
http://parapublishing.com/sites/para/information/promote .cfm


## FOREIGN, RIGHTS

SELLING FOREIGN RIGHTS
--Clint Greenleaf, CEO of Greenleaf Book Group, LP www.greenleafbookgroup.com or 512-891-6100

If you're exploring selling the foreign distribution rights to your title, you can find listings of international publishers to solicit through International Literary Marketplace (by subscription at literarymarketplace.com), or consider working through PMA's Virtual Foreign Rights Book Fair (http://www.pma-online.org/pmafair). Be forewarned that gathering the contacts and communicating with overseas publishers is extremely time-consuming and logistically difficult due to time zones and language barriers. Consider contracting a literary agent for this purpose to capitalize on their contacts, their knowledge of foreign distribution rights market trends, and their experience with the details of such contracts

EXPORTS/FOREIGN RIGHTS: Selling U.S. books abroad shows you how to expand your markets by selling directly to foreign readers, using an exporter in the U.S., contracting with a foreign distributor, and selling subsidiary rights to foreign publishers, with variations, such as international book packaging, co-production, and format rights. Special sections cover options, taxes, shipping, agents, the Frankfurt Book Fair, and more. Exports expand your market, while foreign rights are frosting on your publishing cake: They bring in revenue while the sale amounts to a significant endorsement for your book. These endorsements help to sell more books at home. Complete with sample contracts, postal rate charts, sample letters, and instructions for locating compatible foreign publishers. Glossary and an Appendix full of resources.
ISBN 1-56860-035-6; 35 pages. See
http://parapublishing.com/sites/para/information/promote.cfm and scroll down.

SELLING BOOKS IN THE UNITED STATES, a Guide for Foreign Publishers lists six ways to establish a presence in the U.S. and suggests foreign publishers promote books just as U.S. publishers do: With book reviews, news releases and, if appropriate to the title, with a limited amount of direct mail advertising. Details and resources. This Report is not for U.S.-based publishers.
Document 634, 7 pages. See
http://parapublishing.com/sites/para/information/promote.cfm and scroll down.

RIGHTS ALERT
http://www.PublishersWeekly.com/RightsAlert

FOREIGN DISTRIBUTION. If you're exploring selling the foreign distribution rights to your title, you can find listings of international publishers to solicit through International Literary Marketplace (by subscription at literarymarketplace.com), or consider working through PMA's Virtual Foreign Rights Book Fair (http://www.pma-online.org/pmafair). Be forewarned that gathering the contacts and communicating with overseas publishers is extremely time-consuming and logistically difficult due to time zones and language barriers. Consider contracting a literary agent for this purpose to capitalize on their contacts, their knowledge of foreign distribution rights market trends, and their experience with the details of such contracts.
—Clint Greenleaf, CEO of Greenleaf Book Group, LP
www.greenleafbookgroup.com

INTERNATIONAL SALES DONE RIGHT. Put your titles in the hands of someone with 17 years experience at the Frankfurt Book Fair who has the right contacts to pitch the appropriate publishers, distributors, booksellers, buyers, agents, representatives, reviewers, and suppliers who attend. Frankfurt is not for amateurs in the book trade and is not a show for aisle wanderers. Godfrey Harris is serious about bringing back deal opportunities. Contact him for details at hrmg@aol.com, For details. www.harrisragan.com

FOREIGN RIGHTS WEBSITES
--Frankfurt Book Fair Rights.
http://www.frankfurt-book-fair.com/
--PMA Rights Service
http://pma-online.org/pmafair/index.cfm
--Rights Alert
http://www.PublishersWeekly.com/RightsAlert

Note: Rightsworld.com shut down in September 2001. SubRights.com closed its doors in 2000

## FORMS

ASK FOR EMAIL ADDRESSES on all your order forms. Then you will be able to communicate with your customers faster and cheaper. We use email for both customer service and promoting new products. To find out all about using email, go to http://www.emailman.com.

DOWNLOADABLE AUTHOR'S QUESTIONNAIRE and marketing planning form from Bob Erdmann. See http://www.bob-erdmann.com/forms.html.

DOWNLOADABLE OFFICE FORMS FROM OFFICE DEPOT. See http://www.officedepot.com/renderStaticPage.do?context= /content&file=/BusinessTools/forms/default.jsp

## FULFILLMENT, BOOK

BOOK FULFILLMENT IS EXPENSIVE AND TIME-CONSUMING. John Huenefeld says shipping books costs 7% to 14% of sales depending upon whether most of the books go out in single packages or by the carton.

BOOK FULFILLMENT: Order Entry, Picking, Packing, and Shipping explains in detail how to set up and run your shipping department. The Report covers order taking (letter openers, credit cards, card terminals, 800 numbers, fax, order services, order forms, and discount structures); order processing (computer hardware and software, shipping labels, short slips, bad cheques, overpayments, invoices, back orders, the Federal Trade

Commission rules, complaints, book return policy, statements and collections); inventory and storage (shipping instructions to printer, book receiving, book returns, inventory control, stacking, and shipping room layout) and book packaging (how to wrap, where to get and how to use shipping bags and cartons, machinery such as tape dispensers, scales, postage meters and bag sealers with sources, using UPS, Direct Sacks and various Postal rates, foreign shipping and customs duty). Then the Report covers the alternatives to in-house fulfillment: using wholesalers, distributors, joint representation, and fulfillment warehouses with a list of those to contact. Complete with forms and shipping rate charts, an action plan and an Appendix full of resources. ISBN 978-1-56860-037-6, 46 pages. See http://www.parapublishing.com/sites/para/information/ful fillment.cfm. Scroll down.

HAVE MORE QUESTIONS ABOUT BOOK FULFILL-MENT AND SHIPPING? See http://www.parapublishing.com/sites/para/information/ful fillment.cfm.

FULFILLMENT & SHIPPING YOUR BOOK. Invoicing, Inventory, Picking, Packing & Shipping. http://parapub.com/sites/para/information/fulfillment.cfm

NEED A FULFILLMENT SERVICE? See the Supplier List at http://parapub.com/sites/para/resources/supplier.cfm

# G

## GHOSTWRITERS

You don't have to be the writer to be the author. Most celebrity books are written by a skilled wordsmith. See *Is There a Book Inside You?*.

NEED A GHOSTWRITER? See the Supplier List at http://parapub.com/sites/para/resources/supplier.cfm

## GOOGLE.COM

GOOGLE.COM TIPS. Markus Allen says, When you use Google®, you can narrow your search of PDF files by adding the phrase "inurl:pdf" (without the quotation marks.) For example: "email marketing" inurl:pdf (add a space after the "g"). After a few seconds, Google provided him with links to thousands of PDF files.

Use Google's print search service to find what authors are saying about any subject. Just type in the key words. See http://print.google.com.

GOOGLE LAUNCHES DESKTOP SEARCH. Google Inc. has announced a free downloadable application that is designed to enable users to search for information on their own computers. See http://www.econtentmag.com/NewsLetters/NewsletterReader.aspx?NewsletterID=245#1

GOOGLE MOVES INTO PRODUCT REVIEWS. Google is combining online reviews into its Froogle shopping-search service, but rather than eliciting new opinions it is aggregating reviews and ratings from around the Web. Get more info on Froogle Product Reviews here.

http://ct.enews.eweek.com/rd/cts?d=186-1435-2-79-66269-159315-0-0-0-1.

GOOGLE PRINT. Put your book on Google. Your book would be purchased in far greater numbers if more people knew about it. Now there is a service that can help more readers discover your book. It's called Google Print from Google, it's easy to use and it is free. It's worth a look at http://www.google.com/bea2005. This tip from Kim Dushinsky at http://MarketAbility.com

# H

---

See the "ParaSite" at http://ParaPub.com

---

# I

## IDIOM

CHECK THE DEFINITION/ORIGIN OF AN IDIOM. For example, Catch-22 originated from a 1961 novel by Joseph Heller, where one bureaucratic regulation is dependent on another, which in turn is dependent on the first. See http://idiomsite.com.

## IMAGES, ILLUSTRATIONS

CLIP ART. See

http://www.clipart.com
http://www.clip-art.com/
http://www.barrysclipart.com/

IMAGE RESOURCE. To find images on the Web, try
http://images.google.com. Google is searching web pages
and finding graphics people have on their websites. This
is not a database of "free" clip art, but you will find out
what is out there and then you can contact the site for
permission to use it.

MAPS.COM IS A MAPPING SERVICE FOR
PUBLISHERS. 120 Cremona Drive, Ste. H, Santa
Barbara, CA 93117; Tel: (805) 685-3100; Fax: (805) 685-
3330. Whether you publish textbooks, special interest,
historical, children, religious, reference, or any other
types of publications, maps may be used to make your
book     more     interesting     and     more     useful.
http://www.maps.com

OVER 500,000 PREMIUM DIGITAL IMAGES. Free
images available. See http://www.jupiterimages.com.

Note: Also see Photography.

**INDEX**

A FREE DIRECTORY OF 200+ FREELANCE
INDEXERS with contact and background information.
See http://www.asindexing.org or contact the American
Society of Indexers at (303) 463-2887 or
info@asindexing.org.

**INSURANCE**

INSURANCE FOR PUBLISHERS; *Protecting Your Book
Company*. The very latest on incorporation, insurance,

indemnity clauses, disclaimers, and other ways to limit your exposure to law suits. Cites cases and legal precedent. Resources section lists insurance companies, attorneys, etc. Document 636, 7 pages.
See
http://parapub.com/sites/para/information/business.cfm
and scroll down

## INTERNET, WEB

DON'T MAIL A BROCHURE; take customers to your website. As authors and publishers, we are often in the middle of a project when the telephone rings. Our reaction is to respond to the call as an interruption when it should be treated as an opportunity. Usually, we greet the caller, ask for a name and address and promise to send a brochure. This is peculiar because here we have a potential customer who needs information to solve a current challenge and we put him or her off for several days—waiting for a mailed brochure. Your brochure is on your website; your website IS your brochure. Ask potential clients to log on while you have them on the telephone and lead them to the information that will help them. A bird in the hand . . .

ELECTRONICALLY TRANSMITTED DISEASES (ETD) continue to proliferate. To check on current viruses, see http://symantec.com.

FIND WHAT WEBSITES ARE LINKED TO YOUR SITE, go to http://www.altavista.com and type in your web address.

MAKE YOUR COMPANY WEBSITE-CENTRIC. Redeploy your brochure and postal money into your website. Websites do not cost additional money; they are paid for with money you used to spend on printing and mailing four-color brochures. Websites often cost less than what you were paying for alternative (21st Century) exposure.

MAKING THE WEB PAY, A SET-UP GUIDE FOR PUBLISHERS shows you how to set up your website to make money and save time—automatically. Examples and descriptions are given for selling books, reports and newsletters on-line with some clever and automatic response mechanisms. Document 629, 6 pages. See http://parapub.com/sites/para/information/promote.cfm and scroll down.

ONLY DOTCOM AND 800 NUMBERS COUNT. Peter Kent recommends .com URLs only. He says that people only think of DotCom; they do not look for you at net, org, edu, cc, etc. Many DotComs are taken so if you have one that matches your company name, you appear to have been around a while.

Similarly, when people see "Toll Free," they think 800. They may be looking at 888 or 877 but their fingers hit 800. We know. There is a jeans manufacturer at 877 (PARAPUB) in Quebec. We get (and pay for) 2-3 calls each day—in French. Want to know if an 800 number is available? Call it.

Shel Horowitz (Grassroots Marketing: Getting Noticed in a Noisy World) reminds us that URLs are "portable" just like toll-free telephone numbers. When you move, the website address may be redirected to your new local Internet Service Provider. With your own URL and toll-free number, your addresses are permanent.

"THE INVENTION OF THE INTERNET IS AS IMPORTANT AS THE INVENTION OF THE GUTENBERG PRESS in 1453. To produce a book then took one monk one year. He wrote it by hand. There were 30,000 books on the continent of Europe. By the year 1500, 50 years later, there were 9 million. No one knew then the Gutenberg press would change the world."

"No one has any idea of the profound changes of the Internet, and its new partnership with the phone."
—Harry Newton of Telecom Library in 1996.
Thanks to Sarah Stambler's *Marketing with Technology News* for these items.

TO TRACK EMERGING ONLINE TRENDS, check the Internet surveys at http://www.nua.ie/surveys.

TO VIEW THE END OF THE WEB, see http://www.1112.net/lastpage.html.

YOU COULD LOSE YOUR WEBSITE ADDRESS (URL) if you have changed your address. If Network Solutions (or other registrar) can't find you at renewal time, you could lose your domain name. Someone else could buy it. Go to http://www.networksolutions.com. Find out your renewal date; see if your address is correct.

WANT TO KNOW HOW THE SEARCH ENGINES WORK? Check http://www.SearchEngineWatch.com.

WHEN FEDEX IS NOT FAST ENOUGH, your media kit should be on your website. Let editors get your news releases, cover images, and other press materials immediately and electronically. Editors are more likely to use review materials that are easy to get and they will thank you. For an example, see http://parapublishing.com/sites/para/resources/pressroom.cfm

WHERE ARE YOU LISTED ON THE WEB? Just type in your name at http://www.search.com and get a list.

WORLDWIDE DOMAIN NAMES. Lists different top-level domain names by code and by country. See http://www.brennerbooks.com/domainnames.html.

## INTERVIEWS

FREE AUDIO INTERVIEWS OF LEADING-EDGE MARKETERS. See http://www.moneyroom.com. Hear the following people speak:

Declan Dunn on affiliate programs
Paulette Ensign on publishing booklets
Rob Frankel on branding
John Kremer on promoting eBooks
Dan Poynter on "The New Book Model"
and many more.

JEFF PAUL INTERVIEWS PAUL HARTUNIAN, free. This is the transcript of a taped interview between Jeff Paul and Paul Hartunian on how to get tens of thousands of dollars worth of free publicity http://prprofits.com/jeffpaul.

## ISBN, SAN, ABI & BIP

THE INTERNATIONAL STANDARD BOOK NUMBER (ISBN) is a worldwide identification system, which has been in use since the late 60s. There is a different ISBN for each edition and each binding of every book so the number's use avoids errors in identifying the books ordered, shipped, received, etc. Publishers are finding that with the increased use of computers in the book industry, this system has become an essential element in the distribution of their books.

Contact the International Standard Book Numbering Agency at R.R. Bowker at http://www.bowker.com for ISBN numbers. Tel: (877) 310-7333. Or, log on to http://www.isbn.org. The cost of the ISBN numbers varies depending on how many numbers you want.

The ISBN people will send you a card bearing your ISBN publisher identifier and a logbook sheet with enough room for listing each edition.

Once you are in the system, you will assign each of your new titles an ISBN suffix yourself. You do not have to start at the beginning of the log; the only requirement is that you assign a different ISBN to each *edition* of each book: softcover, hardcover, audiotape, downloadable, CD, etc.

If you use the first number on the logbook sheet, the "0" at the end of the string will tip off those in the industry that this is a first book.

THE ISBN AGENCY NO LONGER MAILS CARDS with the publisher's prefix. Now they mail or email the log sheets listing the numbers.

THE ISBN WILL LENGTHEN. The International Standard Book Numbering Agency is running out of numbers. Not only are more books being published today, now there is a greater need as unique numbers are being applied the audiotapes, eBooks, downloadable editions, print-on-demand versions, etc. Effective January 1, 2006, the ISBN will grow from 10 to 13 digits. Check out the ISBN converter at http://www.PublishingGame.com.

ADVANCED BOOK INFORMATION is another Bowker service. By filling out their ABI form, your book will be listed in *Books in Print* and several other specialized directories. *Books in Print* is published in October of each year and is the most important directory.

Contact the ABI Department, R.R. Bowker Co., 121 Chanlon Rd., New Providence, NJ 07974; Tel: (800) 521-8110 or (732) 464-6800 or (732) 665-2882 and request and a half dozen ABI forms. There is no charge. Or get one online at http://www.bowker.com.

You should fill out an ABI form about six months before your book comes off the press, but don't be too anxious. On your first book, wait until you are about to ship your boards off to the printer. Some new publishers act prematurely; they list the book and then never get into print. Your "publication date" will probably be six months away anyway, as discussed in Chapter Seven of *The Self-Publishing Manual.* Code your address on the ABI forms (see the discussion in Chapter Seven).

Always use the ABI guidebook when filling out the ABI form. Some of the questions may mislead a person not familiar with publishing terminology.
Once enrolled in the ISBN system, you can go online and update or change your listings.

NEW CONTACT INFORMATION FOR THE ISBN AGENCY. The toll-free number is (877) 310-7333; the 800 and 908 numbers have been discontinued. For the current fee structure, see
http://www.bowker.com.
http://www.isbn.org.

TO FILL OUT ADVANCE BOOK INFORMATION FORMS ON LINE, you must (re) register with Bowker at http://www.bowkerlink.com. Then fill in the form at

http://www.bowkerlink.com/corrections/bip/itemsearch.as
p.

WHEN FILLING OUT THE ADVANCED BOOK
INFORMATION (ABI) FORM for *Books In Print*, do not
leave the "Primary Subject of Book" section up to Bowker.
Check BIP and a librarian for the proper subject
headings. You want people to be able to locate your book
when they are searching BIP by *subject*.

CHANGING BIP. Have you changed the subtitle, price or
page count of your book? No worries, you may change
your listing in Book in Print at
http://www.bowkerlink.com/corrections/bip/itemsearch.as
p

UPDATING BIP LISTINGS. Use the online change
forms. Go to http://www.bowkerlink.com, click on
Add/Update in Books in Print and the Publishers
Authority Database. Register and Bowker will email you
your USERNAME and PASSWORD in a couple of days.
Then you will be able to submit your ABI Form (list new
titles) and change listings.

Warning, it will probably take you several discouraging
tries to figure out the form. But the online system is
faster and gives you more control over your listing.
Challenges or questions? Call Bowker at (813) 855-4635
or toll-free at (888) 269-5372.

USING THE BOWKERLINK PUBLISHER ACCESS
SYSTEM. BowkerLink is a F^REE online access system
that provides you with an automated tool to add titles to
*Books In Print*® as well as update any records that are
already listed. Use BowkerLink to submit forthcoming
title information to *Books In Print*® 180 days before

publication and inform them of updates as soon as they occur. Listings are free.

1. Go to: www.bowkerlink.com. Click on "For Books In Print and Publishers Authority Database".

2. If you are registered on BowkerLink, enter your Username and password. Click on "Login". Go to step 4.

3. If you are a NEW USER, click on "Register". Read the Statement of Use and click on "I Agree" if you wish to continue to register. Enter your publisher name and click "Search". Locate your publisher name, click on it to access the registration form, fill in the form and click "Submit". Include your PUBLISHER NUMBER on the registration form to expedite processing. Your USERNAME and PASSWORD will be e-mailed back to you and will be validated for use within three business days. Follow steps 1 and 2 to logon to BowkerLink.

4. To view a complete list of your titles in the Books In Print database, click on the "Search" button. Click on the "red triangle" to view the complete record. You may update your information by adding, deleting, or typing over the existing information. After changes are made, click on "Finish and Save".

STANDARD ADDRESS NUMBER. The SAN identifies each separate address of every firm in the book publishing industry from publishers to wholesalers to libraries to bookstores. SANs sort out the billing and shipping addresses and help to determine which "Book Nook" an order is going to.

A SAN may be requested when you apply for an ISBN. The seven-digit number should be printed on all stationery, purchase orders, invoices, etc. You can get an application at http://www.bowkerlink.com.

# J

# K

## KITS, INFO, MEDIA

FOR LENGTHY LISTS OF RESOURCES, see the three new InfoKits on our website. They have several pages of tips and leads on writing, production, and promotion. Just request one or more "Free InfoKit"; see buttons on the left at

http://parapub.com/sites/para/resources/infokit.cfm

MEDIA KITS cost a great deal to produce and send and most go immediately into the round file. A far better solution is to set up a Press Room on your website with all the media kit materials. Then use email to invite the working press to your Press Room. Let them click through to retrieve news releases, cover art, sidebar info, and so on. For an example, see

http://parapublishing.com/sites/para/resources/pressroom. cfm.

# L

## LARGE PRINT BOOKS

Some of our books are also available in large print editions. Larger print is designed for the visually

impaired, people with reading disabilities and people learning English as a second language. See
http://www.amazon.com/exec/obidos/tg/detail/-/1568600887
http://www.amazon.com/exec/obidos/tg/detail/-/1568601107/
For information on how you can turn your book into large print editions and get them up on Amazon, see Document 642 at
http://parapub.com/sites/para/resources/allproducts.cfm
And for information on producing and selling eBooks at Amazon, see Document 615.

## LEGAL HELP, LAWYERS

INTELLECTUAL PROPERTY ATTORNEYS. See the Supplier List at
http://parapub.com/sites/para/resources/supplier.cfm And
http://parapub.com/sites/para/information/access.cfm?isbn=Document%20113&qty=1&isdl=1

PUBLISHING LAW
http://www.publaw.com
http://www.ivanhoffman.com

PUBLIC LENDING RIGHT (PLR) is the right of authors and other creators to receive payment for the free lending or other use of their works in libraries. See
http://www.plrinternational.com/

## LIBRARIES

FRIENDS OF THE LIBRARY/USA is very active in supporting libraries AND authors. They have been very helpful to us in getting exposure for our authors. They often have their own booth at local county fairs and allow local authors to use their booth at no cost to autograph and sell books. They also have a database that Small or Independent publishers can submit their company info to and get their authors into the database for libraries to contact them and invite them to do book signing/reading events at libraries. We of course have found libraries to be wonderful at getting our authors media attention in newspapers and on radio.

A publisher can go to this link and fill out the form for their authors.

https://cs.ala.org/publicprograms/authorlibrary/publisher.html

—Pam Schwagerl, Tsaba House, www.TsabaHouse.com

LIBRARIES GOING ELECTRONIC. U.S. and Canadian libraries are increasingly giving patrons the option of digital books and audiobooks. In almost all cases patrons must access the eBooks and eAudios from their own computer, rather than on library equipment. Many publishers are already supplying libraries through www.OverDrive.com. Recorded Books and Audible.com are other large-volume suppliers players in the audiobook field.

—Judy Byers, AudioCP Publishing & Consulting, http://www.audiocp.com/; Tel: 541-261-2412; jbyers@audiocp.com

LIBRARIES USUALLY HONOR PATRONS' REQUESTS. Ask your friends around the country to request your book by dropping a note in the suggestion box at their local public library. Then many people will see your book and send for their own copy. The more books you get out there, the more books you will sell.

LIST OF THE TOP 1000 TITLES OWNED BY MEMBER LIBRARIES—the intellectual works that have been judged to be worth owning by the "purchase vote" of libraries around the globe. See http://www.oclc.org/research/top1000/default.htm

ONLINE LIBRARY. See
http://www.bartleby.com/reference.

## LISTSERVS, FORUMS & ONLINE DISCUSSION GROUPS

LISTSERVS. There are four general and several specific discussion groups for authors and publishers. Ask a question and a lot of wonderful, knowledgeable people will answer; this is inexpensive consulting. Subscribe at

PUB-FORUM. http://www.pub-forum.net/
SELF-PUBLISHING.
http://finance.groups.yahoo.com/group/self-publishing/
PUBLISH-L. http://www.publish-l.com/
SMALLPUBCIVIL.
http://finance.groups.yahoo.com/group/smallpub-civil/

Fiction_L. http://www.webrary.org/rs/flmenu.html
Ind-e-pubs. eBooks. http://www.ind-e-pubs.com/
http://groups.yahoo.com/group/ebook-community/
POD Publishers
http://finance.groups.yahoo.com/group/pod_publishers/
Publishing Design
http://groups.yahoo.com/group/publishingdesign/
Book Signings/Mini Seminars.
http://groups.yahoo.com/group/booksigners/
Copy Law. http://groups.yahoo.com/group/copyright-future/

DISCUSSION GROUPS. Promote your book by participating in related email discussion groups. For a directory of listservs and groups, see http://www.liszt.com and http://groups.yahoo.com.

THE MOST LITERATE CITIES. How does your area compare? See http://www.uww.edu/cities.

WRITING          DISCUSSION          FORUMS.          See http://www.freelancewriting.com/yabbprivate/yabb/YaBB.cgi

## LOGO

HOW IMPORTANT IS IT TO HAVE A PUBLISHER LOGO?
--Kathi Dunn, Dunn+Associates Design,
http://www.dunn-design.com

Today's logo can be traced back to ancient China where artists and craftsmen marked their work with a distinctive pictorial symbol. In the industrialized age these personal marks evolved into trademarks which were protected by law. Your logo not only marks your products and your company but it also serves as a signature for your events. A strong logo instantly communicates an identity in a single image. It must have style. It must be timeless, appropriate and unique. It must be readable when larger than a billboard or smaller than a postage stamp, in one color or in full-color. A publisher logo has to be effective on book's spine - a small, less than half-inch space. And think about adding a tag line and how you can interchange tag lines for specific targeted genres. Remember, your logo is often the public's first contact with your company and helps establish that all-important first impression. Your logo is essentially the cornerstone of your brand-building efforts as a publisher.

LOGO PLACEMENT
--Robert Howard. www.bookgraphics.com

Most books in a book store are shelved with spines out.

Although your logo may not be well known, it could help draw attention to your cover by virtue of it's color or shape.

# M

## MAGAZINES

GETTING COVERAGE IN MAGAZINES, newspapers and newsletters for your books. News releases and article. See http://parapub.com/sites/para/information/promote.cfm#sr newsrelease. For a list of periodicals, see http://parapub.com/sites/para/resources/maillist.cfm For an example and a paint-by-the-numbers outline on how to construct a dynamite news release, see http://parapub.com/sites/para/resources/allproducts.cfm

## MAILINGS

ABOUT 15% OF U.S. CONSUMERS HAVE ASKED TO HAVE THEIR ADDRESS REMOVED FROM MAILING LISTS. They just contacted DMA.

1. Junk Mail: Send your name, address, and include your signature in a letter or postcard to:

Direct Marketing Association
Mail Preference Service
P.O. Box 9008
Farmingdale, NY 11735-9008

2. Annoying Telephone Calls: Send your name, address, telephone number, and signature in a letter or postcard to:

Direct Marketing Association
Telephone Preference Service
P.O. Box 9008
Farmingdale, NY 11735-9008

MAILING TO ADDRESSES FROM TELEPHONE DIRECTORIES ON CD CAN BE EXPENSIVE. The addresses rarely include suite numbers and often the mail carriers will not bother to tote the mail to apartment and office buildings without the exact address.

NO SALES TAX. California's taxing authorities have determined we do not have to collect the sales tax on mailing list rentals when the lists are on one-across peel-and-stick labels. Lists are only taxable when supplied on magnetic tapes.

THE BEST MONTHS TO MAKE PROMOTIONAL MAILINGS are in January, February, October, August, November and then September, in that order according to the Direct Marketing Association. Do not make promotional mailings after November 15; people are too busy with the holidays to consider your offer. Let all promotions accumulate and drop them on January 2.

THE U.S. POSTAL SERVICE HANDLES 41% OF THE WORLD'S MAIL. Japan is a distant second with 6% according to *The Wall Street Journal.*

YOUR CUSTOMERS ARE MOVING. Twenty-four percent of the U.S. population moves every year; 40 million address changes are submitted to the Postal Service annually. Of those, 84% are moves with a forwardable address, leaving 16% who disappear. It takes four to six weeks to get a change into the Postal Service's National Change of Address (NCOA) system. By that time nearly five million more people have moved.

## MAILING LISTS

WHERE TO SEND REVIEW COPIES AND NEWS RELEASES. Advertising space is expensive. Editorial space is free. Use these lists to send review copies to magazines, newsletters, ezines, special contacts, and newspapers with subject-specific and book review columns. Review copies and news releases are your least expensive and most effective form of book promotion. For a current list of magazines and counts, see
http://parapub.com/sites/para/resources/maillist.cfm
Here is a list to show you what is available:

| Count | Description |
|-------|-------------|
| 24 | Accounting magazines |
| 35 | Advertising magazines |
| 33 | African American magazines |
| 5 | Almanacs |
| 15 | Native American magazines |
| 25 | Antique magazines |
| 20 | Architecture magazines |
| 318 | Arts/literary/poetry |
| 117 | Automobile magazines |
| 333 | Aviation magazines (73 foreign) |
| 30 | Banking magazines |
| 28 | Boats/boating magazines |
| 12 | Home-business magazines |
| 893 | Business Magazines (62 foreign) |
| 113 | Magazines for children |
| 81 | Book, etc., columnists. |
| 283 | Computer/Web Magazines and n/l |
| 52 | Construction/home Magazines |

| | |
|---|---|
| 9 | Consulting magazines |
| 386 | Consumer Magazines (24 fgn.) |
| 296 | Cooking Magazines & columns |
| 77 | Counter culture, new age |
| 24 | Direct mail advertising Magazines |
| 13 | Economics magazines |
| 306 | Education magazines |
| 35 | Electronics & video |
| 42 | Energy magazines |
| 167 | Entertainment magazines |
| 164 | Environmental Magazines & cols |
| 29 | Expert witness/forensics Magazines |
| 2585 | Retail buyers of Expert Witness Handbook |
| 154 | Farming & gardening Magazines |
| 99 | Financial magazines |
| 214 | Physical Fitness magazines |
| 16 | Gambling magazines. |
| 47 | Gay & Lesbian magazines |
| 14 | Gift magazines |
| 27 | Magazines for the disabled |
| 571 | Health magazines |
| 200 | Hobby & crafts magazines |
| 71 | Home decorating/remodeling |
| 55 | Horse magazines |
| 53 | Humor magazines |
| 36 | Industrial magazines |
| 29 | Insurance magazines |
| 163 | Legal magazines for attorneys |
| 49 | Magazines for librarians |
| 124 | Lifestyle columns |
| 88 | Management magazines |
| 105 | Magazines for the media |
| 107 | Medical magazines |
| 40 | Magazines for men |

617    Military (Base papers, magazines for retired personnel & mil. Magazines) (168 foreign)

109    Military attaches at foreign Embassies

214     Air Force, Navy, Marine & CG libraries
73      Motorcycle magazines
75      Film/movie magazines
97      Music magazines
377     New age magazines and contacts
6       Magazines-nonprofit organizations
21      Nursing magazines/newsletters
22      Office magazines
86      Outdoor magazines
73      Parachute & skydiving magazines
1688    Newspapers with book review & features columns. (472 foreign.)
93      Alternative newspapers.
138     Parenting magazines
73      Pet magazines
28      Photography magazines
60      Law enforcement & correctional officers
112     Political magazines
318     Magazines for book publishers
59      Real estate magazines
31      Relationship magazines
487     Religious magazines
175     Magazines for salespeople
263     Science magazines (13 foreign)
247     Seniors: agazines for older people
16      Sewing magazines
11      Sex abuse magazines
102     Singles magazines & n/l
15      Social service magazines
457     Sports and leisure magazines
64      Magazines for youths/teens
372     Travel magazines & travel columns (10 foreign)
24      Trucking magazines
57      Career magazines
187     Magazines for women

(Counts are constantly changing as we add to and correct the lists)

## OTHER LISTS

ALTERNATIVE NEWSWEEKLIES.
See: http://www.newpages.com/NPGuides/newswkly.htm

ANTIQUARIAN, SPECIALTY, AND USED BOOK SELLERS DIRECTORY lists 5,261 book dealers and what they want. Check the subject index and send your brochure to appropriate stores. For example, we sent our catalog of parachute books to all the aviation and military book stores. The $85, 863-page directory is available from Omnigraphics, Penobscot Building, Detroit, MI 48226. Tel: (800) 234-1340.

BOOKSTORE DIRECTORY, complete with URLs, email addresses and descriptions.
http://www.bookweb.org/bookstores.

CELEBRITY LISTS. Largest online database with celebrity contact information. http://www.Celebrity-Addresses.com. Also see *Blurbs for Your Books*, Document 609 at
http://parapub.com/sites/para/information/produce.cfm.
Scroll down.

EZINE LISTS
http://www.emailuniverse.com
http://www.ezinehub.com

FIND NEWSPAPERS all over the world, see
http://www.esperanto.se/kiosk/engindex.html. The listings include links to the newspapers' websites.

FOR A LIST OF 9,000 LIBRARIES AND 1500 NEWSPAPERS, see http://www.acclaimed.com/helpful/lib-add/htm

GET LIST OF 188 LIBRARIES hand-picked for their likelihood to buy small press publications. They all have book-purchasing budgets of over $500,000, and many have literary or small press special collections. There is a mix of university and major public libraries, so it is unlikely many of the addresses will change. Visit Tom Person's website at http://www.laughingbear.com/library.html

MAGAZINES. Looking for in-depth information on a particular magazine, journal or newsletter? Look it up at http://www.PubList.com.

NOTE TO LIST RENTERS. See http://parapub.com/sites/para/resources/allproducts.cfm

PARENTING MAIL LIST. More than 250 magazines, newsletters, etc. $25. Book Peddlers, Tel: (800) 255-3379; http://www.BookPeddlers.com.

TRAVEL AND FAMILY MAILING LISTS: magazines, newsletters, writers, associations, travel bookstores, zoos, etc. Contact Carousel Press, Tel: (510) 527-5849.

U.S. NEWSPAPERS. U.S. publications are listed by state. International publication lists also available. See Cyberpaper Boy. http://www.cyberpaperboy.com.


**LISTS, RADIO & TV**

For sending media fliers and review books. For a current list of magazines and counts, see

http://parapub.com/sites/para/resources/maillist.cfm
Here is a list to show you what is available:

Count  Description
1554   Radio talk shows & book programs. (37 foreign)
442    TV talk shows & book programs
6      TV news programs


GETTING ON RADIO AND TV. An Author's Radio
Checklist: http://www.CelebrateLove.com/radio.htm

RADIO-TV INTERVIEW REPORT (RTIT). Get
interviews with no effort by advertising in this trade
magazine for 4,000 broadcast producers.
http://www.FreePublicity.com/info227.htm


## LISTS, WRITING & PUBLISHING

For a current list of lists and counts, see
http://parapub.com/sites/para/resources/maillist.cfm
Here is a list to show you what is available:

Count  Description

**Writing business**
211    Magazines for writers
176    Writing clubs and assns
340    Writers' conferences
98     People who type manuscripts

**Publishing business**
546    Literary agents
1153   BEA Book Fair exhibitors
38     Book store associations
212    New Age bookstores

36      Travel bookstores
1254    Bookstores. (117 foreign)
143     Book clubs
1185    Book wholesalers, distributors, exporters (315 foreign)
95      Book fairs
136     Book printers
690     Catalogs that carry books
240     Book chain stores
17      Chain stores (non book)
25      State ctrs for the book
26      Direct mail copy writers
106     Fulfillment companies
30      Graphic arts assoc.
55      Publishers of law books
88      Libraries in Canada
833     Public libraries in U.S.
278     Mailing list brokers
232     Aviation museums
47      Printing associations
155     Book promotion companies (PR people)
401     Publishing associations
31      Attorneys specializing in media law
163     Publishing consultants
672     Poynter's book workshop grads
90      Remainder book dealers
95      Sales reps to bookstores
616     Professional speakers who have written books

## MANUSCRIPT & BOOK EVALUATION

Communication Unlimited, Gordon Burgett. P.O. Box 6405, Santa Maria, CA 93456. Tel: (805) 937-8711. Fax: (805) 937-3035; email: Gordon@sops.com. He will evaluate your manuscript for readability and salability.

## MARKETING, HELP

BOOK MARKETING WORKS, LLC. Brian Jud, 50 Lovely Street, P.O. Box 715, Avon, CT 06001. Tel: (800) 562-4357. Fax: (203) 729-5335. Brian sells books to non-bookstore markets—corporations, discount stores, warehouse clubs, airport stores, and the military. He also offers marketing planning and media training workshops. http://www.bookmarketing.com; brianjud@bookmarketing.com.

CYPRESS HOUSE, Cynthia Frank, 155 Cypress Street, Suite 123, Fort Bragg, CA, 95437-5401. Tel: (707) 964-9520; (800) 773-7782; Fax: (707) 964-7531; Cynthia@cypress.com; http://www.cypresshourse.com Production and promotion services for publishers. Personalized and reasonable.

ELLEN REID'S BOOK SHEPHERDING, a division of Smarketing LLC, 510 Castillo, Suite #301, Santa Barbara, CA 93101; Tel: (805) 884-9911; Fax: (805) 884-9911; ellen@bookshep.com; www.bookshep.com. Ellen Reid provides consulting, coaching and collaboration services to authors who want to professionally publish their own books. She also helps them create the solid foundation of their own small press from which they may effectively position themselves and launch their books.

INK TREE LTD., Box 51152 BPO, Calgary, AB, T3K 3V9, Canada. Tel: (403) 295-3898. Publicity, Consulting & Target Market Book Sales. http://www.InkTreeMarketing.com

ONE-ON-ONE BOOK PRODUCTION & MARKETING. Carolyn Porter and Alan Gadney; 7944 Capistrano Avenue; West Hills, CA 91304; Tel: (818) 340-6620, Fax: (818) 340-6770; onebookpro@aol.com.

The single source for all your publishing and marketing needs (over 30 years of publishing experience). Services include editing, cover and page design, typesetting, printer bidding, creation of sales and promotional materials, full marketing and promotion services, including marketing and promotion to bookstores, libraries, distributors, wholesalers, reviewers, online booksellers and listing sites, foreign rights sources, book exhibit, and co-op marketing programs.

SHERRI ROSEN PUBLICITY, 15 Park Row, Suite 25C, New York, NY 10038; Sherri@SherriRosen.com; http://www.SherriRosen.com. Her first self-published client was on the *New York Times* Bestseller List for 63 weeks.

## MARKETING, BOOKS.

ANY PUBLISHER WHO SAYS HE OR SHE CAN PREDICT WHICH BOOKS WILL SELL, has not been in the industry very long. But gut instinct can be balanced with sound financial analysis to make better decisions. *Financial Feasibility in Book Publishing* by Robert Follett presents a step-by-step method for evaluating the financial future of new book projects. It has worksheets, guidelines, projection methods, rules of thumb, and estimating methods with explanations to help you determine if your book will make money. All new second revised edition. Highly recommended. ISBN 1-56860-026-7, 39 pages. See http://parapublishing.com/sites/para/information/business .cfm and scroll (way) down. Note that this report may be downloaded and printed out right now. You do not have to wait for postal delivery or pay shipping charges.

BOOK PROMOTION RESOURCES. For pages of vitally important promotion ideas, tips, leads and resources, see http://parapub.com/sites/para/resources/infokit.cfm

BOOKS 201: BOOK PROMOTING, MARKETING & DISTRIBUTING. The advanced course on selling books. If you are a publisher or published author, this power-packed intensive course will accelerate your sales, propel your book up the charts, and assure your future. Learn the secrets of non-traditional book sales, electronic promotion, and promoting with articles. Automating your promotion will save you time and money. See http://parapub.com/sites/para/speaking/speechdesc.cfm.

GET YOUR CORE MESSAGE THROUGH TO YOUR TARGET MARKET. If you're not happy with your marketing results, you might want to try seven quick, low cost steps. You may not have to bring in the big guns after all. See http://www.paullemberg.com/7StepsCoreMessage.html.

LOWER YOUR MARKETING COSTS. Shel Horowitz can tell you how to best market your book for the least amount of money. View his site at http://www.frugalmarketing.com.

MARKETING ASSOCIATION. If you want an association that will keep you up to date on all the latest happenings in the online information marketing world, check out http://www.netaim.info. You will have access to advanced Internet experts and the newest technologies. Tom Antion and Gayle Carson are the co-founders and a weekly newsletter and monthly teleseminar are included in your membership.

MARKETING PLAN FOR BOOKS. Books are unique products; selling them requires an individualized plan. There is only one report that will take you through the important steps. *Book Marketing: A New Approach* is a low-cost marketing plan for your book. It describes book trade distributors and lists the types of books they specialize in. Then it shows you how to approach them. The Report leads you through a three-step plan for selling direct to the customer, a five-step plan for selling to bookstores, a seven-step plan for libraries, all the subsidiary rights, and our specialty: the more lucrative non-traditional markets. You will discover how to sell your books to catalogs, as premiums, as fundraisers, to specialty stores, etc. This step-by-step plan will ensure you have completely covered every possible market. An absolute gold mine of book promotion references and sources. Start your book promotion with this Special Report. ISBN 1-56860-029-1, Special Report, 76 pages. See http://parapublishing.com/sites/para/information/promote .cfm and scroll down.

MARKETING WITHOUT MEGABUCKS Shel Horowitz, well-known copywriter and author of Marketing Without Megabucks: How to Sell Anything on a Shoestring, has a book called Grassroots Marketing: Getting Noticed in a Noisy World. When I read a galley, I was so impressed, I gave him a testimonial for the cover.

The book is crammed with useful information for publishers and other small-business owners about how to lower the cost of marketing while increasing effectiveness. It should save the average publisher many thousands of dollars every year. To learn more, visit http://www.frugalmarketing.com.

THE LATEST MARKETING METHODS from On-line Marketing University. See http://www.e-comprofits.com/howtoarticles.html.

1001 WAYS TO MARKET YOUR BOOK. John Kremer is the ultimate researcher, detective, and packrat. With his ear to the ground, his eyes in the media and his nose in the Net, he ferrets out all the inside information and details on places to promote and sell books. Then he generously shares it in 1001. Kremer's book is every publisher's most important resource. The successful ones keep the latest edition next to their dictionary within immediate reach. You can have this treasure too. Invest in it now.

Kremer writes from detailed research and hard-earned experience. He covers advertising, promotion, distributors, bookstores, book design, libraries, spin-offs, and more. In fact, there is little he does not cover and cover well. http://www.bookmarket.com

NEED SOMEONE TO HELP YOU WITH BOOK MARKETING AND PROMOTION? See the Supplier List at http://parapub.com/sites/para/resources/supplier.cfm

MARKETING, PROMOTING & DISTRIBUTING YOUR BOOK. Wholesalers & Distributors. Book reviews, news releases, autographings, interviews, book fairs, export & foreign rights. http://parapub.com/sites/para/information/promote.cfm

**MERCHANT STATUS & CREDIT CARDS**

FREE MERCHANT CARD DECALS AND SIGNS: Visa, MasterCard, Discover and American Express. http://www.AmericanExpress.com/decals. These are useful for book fairs and BOR (Back Of the Room) sales when speaking. (You must have an Amex account to get the decals and signs).

DEBTSMART, a free ezine from Scott Bilker covers credit cards, debt, and money. To contribute or subscribe, see http://www.DebtSmart.com.

MERCHANT STATUS: Credit Cards for Publishers. Book publishers need Merchant Status so they may accept Visa, MasterCard, and other credit cards from their customers. Credit card use will increase sales and increase the size of the sale while cutting down on collection challenges. This report will show you the shortcuts to merchant status and the expensive pitfalls to avoid. Document 641, 11 pages. See http://parapublishing.com/sites/para/information/business .cfm and scroll down.

THERE ARE TWO BASIC KINDS OF MERCHANT STATUS: traditional (to sell from a storefront) and eCommerce (to sell from a website).

If you want to sell from your website AND have Real Time credit card processing, you need an eCommerce account. Several companies offer the service. CyberCash, one of the best known, has a setup charge and then charges $.20 per transaction.

For traditional (walk-in/card-swipe or telephone order-mail order) merchant status, you need a computer program such as QuickBooks, ICVerify or PC/Mac Authorize. Do not get the terminals and printers; they are older, slower and noisy. For information on the programs, contact (800) 666-5777.

## MILITARY BOOKS

WAR EXPERIENCES. Books about military service, particularly books about World War II, are among the most popular in the country right now. Word Association welcomes manuscripts and can help you write your story. http://www.wordassociation.com/military-book-publisher.html

## MILITARY MARKET

THE MILITARY MARKET consists of more than 11 million active, retired, dependents, etc., who buy over $10 billion worth of goods each year. Books are sold through more than 500 exchange stores; they are also purchased for service use. For example, Dan Poynter's parachute manuals are purchased for use in military parachute lofts. For more information on this lucrative outlet, see Selling Books to the Military Market by Michael Sedge. See. http://parapublishing.com/sites/para/information/promote .cfm. Scroll down to Document 637.

# N

## NEW AGE BOOKS

NEW AGE. Millions of Americans are interested in the "new age" lifestyle and tap into its marketplace. Sales of products and services in alternative health continue to increase every year.

NEW AGE BOOKS; Resources for Writing, Producing and Promoting Books on metaphysics, the occult, and new thinking. Provides the leads and resources you need for more information. Document 617, 3 pages. See http://parapub.com/sites/para/information/access.cfm?rep ort=617&refpage=promote.html.

## NEW BOOK MODEL

SIMULTANEOUS PUBLISHING. The New Book Model is not just self-publishing. It covers all the bases and is the best route for anyone with a manuscript. New typesetting and printing technology allows an author to produce 500 softcover books at a very reasonable price. Then finished books are sent to 2-3 selected agents, 2-3 are sent to publishers with track records for that type of book, 3-400 are sent for review to genre-specific magazines, 4-5 are sent to specialized books clubs, about 10 are sent to foreign publishers suggesting translation, and a handful are sent to opinion molders in your field. If an agent or publisher comes in with a good offer, you should sell out. If not, your bases are covered: Your book is out for review and the orders are starting to come in. So, the New Book Model saves time, inventory space, and money while testing the market. You won't print more books until after they are sold.

The New Book Model, Text.
http://parapub.com/sites/para/resources/newbook.cfm

The New Book Model, Audio.
http://www.jackstreet.com/jackstreet/RR.Newbookmodel.cfm
(Wait for the sound to load)

BUY DIGITAL; analog is history. Whether you are in the market for a cell phone, voice recorder, television set, or any electronic device, look at digital models first. Then look for models without moving parts; they use more energy (batteries). For example, the cassette tape is history. Spinning minidisks could be next. Voice recorders are using stationary flash memory cards.

MOVING FROM A PRINT CULTURE TO AN ELECTRONIC CULTURE. According to media expert and author Michael Levine, in the last year, newspaper and publishing stocks in the S&P 500 are down 9%, as readers devote more attention to blogs and media buyers send more dollars to the likes of Google and Yahoo. http://www.LevinPR.com

DOES THE NEW BOOK MODEL WORK? Thousands of published authors say YES! See our Success Stories at http://parapub.com/sites/para/resources/successstories.cfm

**NEWSLETTERS & EZINES**

E-ZINES create repeat impressions. The Publishing Poynters ezine is hosted by SparkList.com.

FREE ARTICLES FOR YOUR E-ZINE OR NEWSLETTER. See http://website101.com/free_ezine_content/

NEWSLETTER PUBLISHING; A Resource Guide provides tips and lists the help you will need to write, produce, publish and promote a newsletter. Document 611, 4 pages. See http://parapub.com/sites/para/information/writing.cfm and scroll down.

NEWSLETTER SCHEDULES. Too many ezines are sent on Mondays and most (smaller/newer) publishers do their reading on weekends. So we try to send Publishing Poynters before the weekend of the publication date.

PUBLICITY HOUND TIPS OF THE WEEK is a free newsletter from media relations expert Joan Stewart. Go to http://www.PublicityHound.com. Her auto responder will send you a bonus copy of "89 Reasons to Send a News Release."

ARTICLE BANK. Articles and quotations (great fillers) that may be used by editors of magazine, newsletters and web sites.
http://parapub.com/sites/para/resources/articlebank.cfm

NEWSLETTER. Publishing Poynters ezine. Full of tips and resources on book writing, publishing and promoting Subscribe, unsubscribe and get past issues.
http://parapub.com/getpage.cfm?file=/news.html

## NEWS RELEASES

CONFINE YOUR NEWS RELEASE TO JUST ONE TOPIC. Covering multiple items and news angles makes your release lose focus and it is hard for an editor to use it.　　　　　　　　　　　　　　　　　　　See
http://www.parapublishing.com/sites/para/information/promote.cfm.

SEND NEWS RELEASES OUT MONTHLY (most periodicals are monthlies) to the lists noted in the Book Review section, above.

HOW TO WRITE A NEWS RELEASE. See
http://www.howipromotemywebsite.com/how-to-write-a-press-release.html
http://www.howipromotemywebsite.com/press-release-links.html
http://www.imediafax.com/tpnr/
http://www.prweb.com/pressreleasetips.php
http://www.IdeaLady.com/publicity.htm
http://www.lunareclipse.net/pressrelease.htm
http://parapub.com/sites/para/information/promote.cfm

http://www.bookmarketingworks.com/marketingservices.htm

NEWS RELEASE DISTRIBUTION SERVICES. See
http://www.24-7pressrelease.com/
http://www.addpr.com/
http://www.arrivenet.com/
http://www.bookcatcher.com/
http://www.click2newsites.com/
http://www.free-press-release.com/
http://www.mediauk.com/
http://www.pressbox.co.uk/
http://www.PressMethod.com/
http://www.press-world.com/
http://www.prfree.com/
http://www.prleap.com/
http://www.zinos.com/
http://www.owt.com/dircon

THE LIFESTYLE EDITOR OF YOUR LOCAL PAPER is much more likely to be interested in you and your book than the book editor. More of the appropriate people you want to reach read the "Lifestyle" section than the "Book" section. Your book is an inspiration to readers and you are an expert on your subject (because you wrote the book). Remember that you are not an author, publisher, or publicist, you are an *information provider*. Contact the Lifestyle editor.

TAKING ADVANTAGE OF THE NEWS. Television news stations are so desperate to fill air time, they will focus on the latest scandal or crisis. With a little imagination, authors can take advantage of this media thirst for stories. Just look for a connection (hook) between the current events and your book.

For example, if you have a book on the geography or history of Florida, you are an expert on that state. You can comment on the political makeup of the (retirement and immigrant) population. Jeff Marx wrote "How to Win a High School Election." He could relate how teens learn about voting, how ballots are counted in high school, why the percentage of voter turnout is higher in high school than after graduation and so on. Christine Harvey published *Can A Girl Run for President?* Her connection is even closer. If you have a book on seniors, wintering, mobile homes, vision, decision-making—well you get the idea.

If you wrote a book, you are an expert in your subject. Now, all you have to do is to use your imagination to connect your subject and book to the breaking news and let the media know you are available.

Paul Hartunian is a master at this. He makes up a list of major TV news programs, morning shows, and Sunday shows and stores them in his computer. Now, when news breaks, he dreams up a hook, alters the news release mentioning his book and faxes it to every show.

Test several potential hooks by telephoning radio and TV call-in shows. Draft your pitches; write them out. Begin by identifying yourself as the author of (your book), then state your observation. Choose your words carefully and refine your observation to sound bites. Then be prepared for questions to explain what you have found. Once you get a good reaction, approach larger shows.

As an author, you were creative enough to write your book. Now, use your creative ability to dream up a connection between it and current events. The media needs you. Your book will thank you.

TIE NEWS RELEASES INTO HOLIDAYS AND OTHER PREDICTABLE EVENTS. The media will be talking about the subject and looking for related material. See John Kremer's *Celebrate Today* and *Chase's Annual Events* for dates but use only the better-known events. http://www.chases.com

FOR AN EXAMPLE and a paint-by-the-numbers outline on how to construct a dynamite news release, see Document 150 (free) at http://parapub.com/sites/para/resources/allproducts.cfm

NEW RELEASE OUTLINE. See Document 160 at

NEED SOMEONE TO WRITE ADS OR NEWS RELEASES? See the Supplier List at http://parapub.com/sites/para/resources/supplier.cfm

## MEDIA

APPROACHING THE MEDIA—Pam Lontos, http://www.PRPR.net

Every contact you make with the media should be considered an interview. They are always listening. Do you have energy in your voice? How do you sound? Are you a fast answerer? Stand when you're on the phone and smile when you talk. Your alertness and excitement will come through in your voice. Even if they say you're on, you can still be cancelled.

PR LEADS LISTS THE STORIES THE MEDIA IS WORKING ON. Contacting a journalist working on a matching story is a fast, easy, and economical way to get your message (with a book mention) into print. See http://www.prleads.com.

REALLY COOL WAY TO PITCH YOUR BOOK TO MEDIA.
-- Kim Dushinski, Partner, MarketAbility.com
www.HowToMarketMyBook.com

SUCCESSFUL PR COVER LETTER & RELEASE SAMPLES. See http://www.bookzonepro.com/insights/articles/article-66.html.

NEWS RELEASE COPY WRITING TIP FROM JAY ABRAHAM. To come up with descriptive terms and buzz words to describe your book, read reviews of similar books at Amazon.com.

WRITING NEWS RELEASES, SALES LETTERS, AND ADS with "Hypnotic Writing." Learn the inner secrets of writing news releases, sales letters, articles, and books that grab readers and hold them with the proven copywriting methods of Joe "Mr. Fire!" Vitale. See his "Hypnotic Writing" e-book online at http://www.hypnoticwriting.com

YOUR WEBSITE SALES COPY should be the same as your book's back cover sales copy. You worked hard on your back cover; why start over? For a FREE paint-by-the-numbers outline of what to put on your back cover, see http://parapublishing.com/sites/para/information/produce.cfm. Scroll down.

TO SEND A NEWS RELEASE TO BUSINESS PERIODICALS via email, log on to this website: http://www.ideasforbusiness.com/direct. Click on one of 1,800 business newspapers or magazines and send your message.

NEWS RELEASES AND BOOK PUBLICITY shows you how to draft news releases and other publicity for your books. After book reviews, news releases are your most effective and least expensive form of book promotion and you may send one out every month. Yet, few publishers use or even know about news releases. Newspaper and magazine editors want to pass on interesting information to their readers. The trick is to draft an interesting news release (tied into your book) that the editor will want to use. Editorial matter is believed; advertising is viewed with skepticism. Do not spend money on advertising when you can use the same effort and less money to send a news release. If you are not sending out a news release on each book every 30 days, get this Report. Step-by-step instructions, paint-by-the-numbers format outlines, many examples and resources are included. See Doc 150. ISBN 978-1-56860-033-8, 34 pages. See http://parapublishing.com/sites/para/information/promote .cfm#bkrev. Scroll down.

PUBLICITY SERVICE. You can write a publicity release and have it sent out without charge or you can increase the distribution by making small donations. It is a great service and very effective. Just go on the net and type http://www.PRweb.com
--Elizabeth Kearney, Kearney & Associates

## NON-TRADITIONAL MARKETS
Selling outside the book trade

ASSOCIATIONS BUY BOOKS FOR RESALE TO THEIR MEMBERS. There are more than 23,000 national associations, 15,000 international associations, and 100,000 regional, state and local associations based in the U.S. Seven out of 10 people in the country are members of at least one association; 25% are members of four or more.

CATALOGS MOVE BOOKS. More than 7,000 mail-order businesses in the U.S. send out 11.8 billion catalogs each year. Many carry books, they buy in large quantities and they are committed to you for the life of the catalog—often a year. Our Document 625, Selling Books to Catalogs reveals how to find the right ones, how to approach them and what you can expect from them. This is one of our top sellers. See http://www.parapublishing.com/sites/para/information/promote.cfm and scroll down.

COOPERATIVE BOOK PROMOTION describes the many programs that enable publishers to join together to lower marketing costs. You will learn about the co-op mail, exhibit, and other programs run by several firms and associations as well as how to set up your own. Complete with an action plan and addresses of over 100 co-op programs. Document 622, 7 pages. See http://www.parapublishing.com/sites/para/information/promote.cfm and scroll down.

DO YOU HAVE A BOOK SUITABLE FOR SALE IN NATIONAL PARKS? Contact: Eastern National, Purchasing Department, 470 Maryland Drive, Suite 1, Fort Washington, PA 19034, (215) 283-6900. Ask for their review copy procedures. They'll send you a list of National parks in the east & information on how to get your books submitted for review and potential acceptance for sale. See http://eParks.com and http://www.easternnational.org.

MOST MUSEUMS HAVE HIGH PERSONNEL TURNOVER due to volunteer help or low pay. Mail to them regularly to remind the new person it is time to (re)order.

SEARCH MORE THAN 20,000 WEB SHOPPING SITES AND MAIL ORDER CATALOGS on the web. Log on to http://www.buyersindex.com. Search for subject-specific catalogs to sell your books and get your catalog of books listed.

SELLING BOOKS THROUGH THE GIFT TRADE. Lists the resources you need for more information: gift shows, magazines, mailing lists, reports and consultants. Document 614, 6 pages See http://www.parapublishing.com/sites/para/information/promote.cfm and scroll down.

THE MAJORITY—53% OF ALL BOOKS—are sold through discount stores, price clubs, drug stores, and other non-bookstores.

WORD OF MOUTH IS TOP SELLER OF BOOKS. According to *The Independent*, "Publishers can spend a fortune promoting their hottest literary discoveries. Bookshops can deploy all their marketing ingenuity to produce imaginative displays. But when the book-buying public comes to choose a new read, it is word of mouth that counts." Next comes author loyalty. To view this publication, See http://enjoyment.independent.co.uk

# O

## OFFICE EQUIPMENT

BUYING OFFICE EQUIPMENT. If you are looking for office equipment, don't forget to check out eBay.   There are also bargains to be found on credit card terminals and lots more.

Some of the items I found on eBay are new, some not. I've also noticed that some of them go for outrageous prices—but there are lots of bargains to be found, too. Do your homework, and you can get one of the good buys. (Then get out of eBay before you find yourself bidding on one of those toys you had when you were a kid, or the baseball card your mom threw away, or....)
—From Cathy Stucker, The Idea Lady
   http://www.IdeaLady.com/bright.htm

## ONLINE SELLING

NATIONAL ACADEMY PRESS PUT 1,700 OF THEIR CURRENT TITLES on the web where they could be read free. Sales shot up 17%. The theory is that surfers browse, as they do in bookstores, and then they buy.

## ORDER PROCESSING & INVOICING

MORE AND MORE PEOPLE USE THE TELEPHONE to order today. If they are paying $.10/minute or less for telephone service, a three-minute call is cheaper than a stamp. Now customers are calling in their book orders for both speed and price.

ORDERING AND TIME ZONES. People who regularly order products by telephone are finding they can sometimes get faster service from suppliers in the Pacific Time zone. Overnight delivery firms, such as FedEx, make their last pickup of the day three hours later in the west than in the east while delivery costs are the same. Customers are finding they can call from the east as late as 8:00 p.m., just make the 5:00 p.m. western pickup, and get delivery by 10:30 the next morning.

SHAM INTERNATIONAL ORDERS ARE ON THE INCREASE. Godfrey Harris reports that U.S.-based websites are finding that some international orders are fraudulent. At Borders.com, 30 to 40 international book orders each day turn out to be shams. Borders' system automatically double-checks orders over $50 for authenticity, but some criminals get around this by submitting multiple small orders. Countries that retailers have found to generate numerous suspect orders include former Eastern bloc nations and Haiti.

## OTHER PROFIT CENTERS: CONSULTING

BRING ATTENTION TO YOUR BOOK BY OFFERING ADVICE. (From A. B. Curtiss, www.abcurtiss.com, who is the author of the book DEPRESSION IS A CHOICE.) I help sales of my book by offering to answer questions online for people as an expert on depression and bi-polar disorder. (I am a board-certified cognitive behavioral therapist). At the end of my specific answer to them personally, I can discreetly offer more general info on my website: www.depressionisachoice.com. Not only do I get people interested in my book, but, equally important, I learn from the questions people ask me how to update and re-target my material for essays and articles. Note: There are several free expert advice sites on the web, such as www.allexperts.com.

COACHING IS A SPECIAL TYPE OF CONSULTING. If you have written a book, you are probably an expert in your subject. As an expert, you are probably qualified to be a coach. Coaching others will add a new revenue stream to your business. For tips on coaching: http://www.schrift.com/tips.htm.

---

⚡️⚡️ Para Publishing.com—Where publishers go for answers.

---

# P

## PACKING, SHIPPING & SUPPLIES

TURN YOUR SHIPPING-ROOM STAMP PAD OVER AT NIGHT to allow the ink to gravitate to the top of the pad.

Also, PUT A FEW DROPS OF VINEGAR in the water tray of your gummed-tape dispenser. It helps the water to cut the glue and makes the tape stickier.

PACKAGING TIP. Clint Greenleaf says, "More and more book industry professionals are considering using sealed air pillows to fill up cartons. These systems run about $3,500 for a basic unit, plus about $.50 per plastic bag. During a staff meeting, one of our associates, Michelle Wotowiec, suggested that we use balloons instead. After a momentary laugh, we realized that this was the idea of the year! You can adjust the size of the balloon without any effort, and all you need is an air compressor or a good set of lungs. We now buy balloons for about $.04, and we're even considering getting our logo on them for orders to bookstores. We've shipped these boxes full of these balloons all over the country and the books arrive in great shape. Tel: (512) 891-6100; www.greenleafenterprises.com

PLACE CLEAR TAPE OVER YOUR SHIPPING LABELS and packing list envelopes to assure they are not scraped off by another carton in transit.

PUT YOUR SHIPPING BAG HEAT SEALER ON A LIGHT TIMER. Then if you forget to turn off the machine at least it will not be on and hot after office hours.

SHRINK WRAP HARDCOVER BOOKS to protect their delicate jackets. If you are shipping in Sealed Air Mail-Lite bags, the jackets will catch and tear on the bubbles. If you use varidepth folder boxes, the shrink-wrap eliminates the need for a protective plastic bag. Since the plastic protection provides a moisture barrier as well as scuff resistance, softcover books should be shrink wrapped too. Ask your printer. The cost is about $.10 per shrink.

PRINT YOUR OWN COLOR SHIPPING LABELS with your inkjet printer on Avery 8163 labels. See http://www.hp.com.

LABEL LAYOUT. To create your own shipping labels from Avery blank stock in MS-Word, click on 'Tools," then "Envelopes and Labels." Click the "Options" button. In the "Label Products" field, find and select Avery. In the "Product Number" field, click on your exact label. Click OK. Then click on "New Document." If you don't see any guidelines on the page, click on "Table" and then "Show Gridlines." From there you can fill in the labels with whatever you like—text, pictures, etc., just as you would with any other document. Then print out a sheet of labels on Avery stock.
—Julie Murkette.

BOOK SHIPPING SUPPLIES. (From Gil Gilpatrick)
http://www.veripack.com

BOOKSTORES ARE A GOOD SOURCE FOR SHIPPING CARTONS. Stores usually get more than they can recycle and disposal is expensive. Check the Dumpster and ask the store manager.

## FREE SHIPPING SUPPLIES.
http://wwwapps.ups.com/using/services/supply
http://supplies.usps.gov/

FREE SHIPPING SUPPLIES from the Postal Service. We ship most of our books and other products via Priority Mail. The rates are good and our customers receive their resources in 2-3 days. We like the larger video boxes from shipping our 5.5 x 8.5 books. You can get all sorts of boxes, tape, envelopes, and labels free and the Postal Service will deliver them. See http://supplies.usps.gov. BTW, no fair using these free supplies to ship via other carriers.

## PACKING BOOKS
--Clint Greenleaf, CEO of Greenleaf Book Group, LP
www.greenleafbookgroup.com or 512-891-6100

If you do your own fulfillment, take the time to pack the books carefully and securely to minimize costly damaged returns. Horror stories abound about the treatment of book shipments through the major shipping companies. If your books are not shrink-wrapped, do not pack them with Styrofoam peanuts because the peanuts can crumble in shipping and bend or lodge in pages, rendering your books un-saleable product that will come back to you.

## PATENTS
http://www.patents.com
http://www.USPTO.gov

## PEN NAME, PSEUDONYM

SHOULD YOU USE A PEN NAME? FREE article from Ivan Hoffman, Esquire. See
http://www.ivanhoffman.com/pennames.html

## PERSONNEL & PAYROLL

HOW MUCH ARE FREELANCE JOURNALISTS BEING PAID? Visit the National Writers Union website at http://www.nwu.org.

PMA RELEASES BOOK INDUSTRY SALARY SURVEY. The document provides publishers at all revenue levels with the means to benchmark the salaries they pay employees in a wide variety of positions with those of their peer publishers.
http://www.pma-online.org/benefits/whitepapers.cfm

## PHOTOCOPYING

WHEN PHOTOCOPYING A NEWSPAPER ARTICLE, place a black sheet of paper behind it. The dark sheet will help minimize ghost characters from the other side of the paper.

## PHOTOGRAPHS

AERIAL PHOTOS. See
http://www.mapmart.com/aerial.htm

NEED TO FIND PHOTOS FOR YOUR NEXT PUBLISHING PROJECT? The free website, PhotoSource International, will not only locate the source of highly specific images, e.g., split-rail, immigrant, explosion, and carnival (over a million listed in the index), but will give you the contact information of the photographer you can deal with directly and negotiate for the use of the picture. Call (715) 248-3800. http://www.photosource.com.

PHOTO CAPTIONS. Put three- to four-line captions under the photos in your ads, brochures, and newsletters. Readers often skip the print, look at the photo, and read the caption. They will go back and read the text if your caption interests them.

--Andrew Linick, The Copyologist.™

PHOTO SHARING SITE. See http://daily.webshots.com

POPULAR, FREE, STOCK PHOTO SITE. Choose from over 100,000 photographs to illustrate your book. http://www.sxc.hu.

STOCK PHOTOS OF CHINA. http://www.greaterchinaphoto.com

SELL YOUR PHOTOGRAPHS. List of 8,500 buyers of photographs at magazine and book publishing companies. See http://www.photosource.com

ROYALTY-FREE STOCK PHOTOS. The top-ten sites. See http://weblogs.about.com/od/writingandcontent/tp/FreeStockPhotos.htm

## PLANS & PLANNING

FOUNDATION. Building a successful book promotion program is like building a house—you must begin with a firm foundation. Your foundation consists of getting a distributor to the bookstores (making your books available to the public) and sending out lots of books for review (to get the customers into the stores). Then you must begin with your news release program. Do not generate interest in your books until they are in the stores. Do not justify inaction by thinking you will start off slowly with small mail-order sales to individuals and build up. Distributors have three selling cycles each year, and they have long lead times. You must get started now.

Get our documents 605 *Locating the Right Distributor*, 612 *BestSellers*, and 620 *Your Book Publishing Calendar*. See http://parapublishing.com/sites/para/information/promote .cfm#promote1 and scroll down.

TALKING ABOUT YOUR BOOK. Not everyone will want to buy your book, but you can get many more sales if you learn how to talk about your book with the 30-second "tell and sell." Also known as an "elevator speech" for the short time you are in an elevator.

Who will buy? Agents, publishers, booksellers, distributors, wholesalers, corporate people, meeting planners, and individuals. They don't have a lot of time. They want the meat of your book in sound bites. Your "tell and sell," like an elevator speech, must be clear, compact, compelling, and commercial.

After you have your sizzling title and know your audience and your book's general and specific benefits, you are ready to create your "tell and sell." Use these elements in it and create one or two sparkling sentences. This task may take many edits —up to fifteen, so be patient with the process. Brainstorm with your friends and associates to get the best mix.
—Judy Cullins. judy@bookcoaching.com

PLANNING, BUSINESS

ASK YOUR PRINTER IF YOU MAY PAY WITH A CREDIT CARD and then use airline-affinity plastic. You will have an extra 29 days to pay and you get a pile of airline points.

BOOK PROFIT & LOSS FORM, free. Download from Bob Erdmann's site.
http://www.bob-erdmann.com/TitleProfit-Loss.xls

BUSINESS PLAN AND MARKETING PLAN OUTLINES. See
http://hometown.aol.com/catspawpress/PubTools.html

FINANCIAL FEASIBILITY IN BOOK PUBLISHING by Robert Follett presents a step-by-step method for evaluating the financial future of new book projects. Worksheets, guidelines, projection methods, rules of thumb, and estimating methods with explanations help you decide whether your book will make money. All new, second revised edition. Highly recommended. ISBN 978-1-56860-026-0, 39 pages. See
http://parapub.com/sites/para/information/business.cfm
and scroll down.

HOW TO SET UP & RUN a Successful Book Publishing Business. Dan Poynter describes his 11-point plan for successfully operating your publishing company. Learn the advantages to being a smaller publisher, why you must publish more than one book—in the same field, the importance of consistent packaging, should you pursue wholesale over retail sales, the secrets of low-cost book promotion and more. Document 624, 7 pages. See
http://parapub.com/sites/para/information/business.cfm
and scroll down.

PERSONAL GOAL PLANNER by the GoalsGuy Gary Ryan Blair. What Are Your Goals? Repetition is the mother of learning and if you're serious about attaining your goals, daily attention is essential. The GoalsGuy's

Personal Goal Planner encourages you to review your mission and legacy and to write daily goals. Gary Ryan Blair, offers a complimentary Personal Goal Planner to the readers of Publishing Poynters. Simply send a request to Gary at Gary@GoalsGuy.com for your goal planner, which will fuel your efforts to achieve an extraordinary life.
Check other free items that are available at http://www.goalsguy.com/Shop/complimentary.php.    Tel: (877) 462-5748.

The GoalsGuy inspires people to live into their full potential through learning resources that make the heart sing, the mind expand, and the spirit soar.

RAISING MONEY TO PUBLISH BOOKS will show you where the money is and how to get it. There are grants, government programs, creative ways to borrow, and lots of good financing advice. If you need money to publish your next book, this report will help you get it. Document 626, 6 pages. See http://parapub.com/sites/para/information/business.cfm. and scroll down.

SELL PRODUCTS, NOT HOURS. You have only 24 hours in each day. Rather than teach a class, multiply your efforts by using the time to write and sell a book. You will serve more people and make more money if you sell products.

THE CYCLE OF A BOOK. A free downloadable form from Bob Erdmann.
http://www.bob-erdmann.com/BookCycle.pdf

WANT TO MAKE DECISIONS BASED ON THE NUMBERS? Kiplinger, the producer of many practical

money-management products, has an online tool section at http://www.kiplinger.com/tools/
with hypertext links to calculators that will help determine what you need for state taxes, retirement, college, and more. Take a look at the list and get definite answers to your questions.
—Jim Zinger

YOUR BOOK PUBLISHING CALENDAR, When to do what. Book publishing is easy but the book trade is unique. This checklist assures you are doing everything correctly, in the right order, and on time. References and resources.
Document 620, 4 pages. See
http://parapub.com/sites/para/information/business.cfm
and scroll down.

## POCKET PC

FOR INFO ON THE POCKET PC, see
http://www.microsoft.com/mobile/pocketpc.

## POSTAL SERVICE

BOOK PUBLISHER'S POSTAL RATE CHART. Print out and post next to your postage meter. See Document 144 at
http://parapub.com/sites/para/resources/allproducts.cfm
For more information on book fulfillment (shipping) see
http://parapub.com/sites/para/information/fulfillment.cfm

FOR A COMPARISON OF MEDIA MAIL AND OTHER RATES, see
http://www.upperaccess.com/bpm.htm

POSTAL RATES. See http://www.USPS.gov

MOVING YOUR BUSINESS? See http://www.usps.com/moversnet.

## POST OFFICE BOXES

SWITCHING P.O. BOXES TAKES TIME. We switched our box nine years ago. We notified everyone—repeatedly—and still some important mail arrives at the old box. The previous box number is printed in more than a million books. When you move, maintain your old address as long as possible.

## PREPRESS

For instructions on getting your book ready for the printer, see *Writing Nonfiction: Turning Thoughts into Books* by Dan Poynter. See http://ParaPublishing.com

FACT CHECK every address before you go to press. We called every number listed in *The Self-Publishing Manual* before we went to press less than a year ago. Now we are preparing the 11th (20th anniversary) edition and about 85% of those listed have moved, changed a fax number or an area code.

## PRICING

TO PRICE YOUR BOOK, see the shelf it will be on in the bookstore. Your book must be priced with the books it will be compared to. The price you put on the back cover has nothing to do with the cost to manufacture.

HOW TO PRICE YOUR BOOK. Selecting the right price for your book is almost as important as selecting the right title for it. Dan Poynter provides you with an easy two-step plan to select the price that will maximize sales—

and profits. He also explains other price-related consid-
erations, such as placement of the price on the back cover,
the price extension in the bar code, why you need an
order blank on the last page of your book, and more.
Document 604, 4 pages. See and scroll down:
http://parapub.com/sites/para/resources/allproducts.cfm

PRICING. If you'd like to charge more but can't explain
why to your prospects, read this article by Paul Lemberg
at the following website:
http://www.paullemberg.com/valueproposition.html

WHAT IS YOUR BOOK WORTH?
—Eric Gelb, http://www.PublishingGold.com

Continually emphasize and highlight the value of what
you're offering. Why should a reader (customer) purchase
your book? What benefits/value does your book offer?
What's in it for them?

THE SUPPLIER PRICING TABLES list the high, low,
and average price for a wide range of services including
writing, editing, scanning, graphic design, DTP layout,
digital photography, prepress, multimedia, and Web
design and development. Nine regional books cover the
United States and Canada. Brenner Information Group,
Tel: (800) 811-4337 Sales@BrennerBooks.com
http://www.brennerbooks.com

## PRINTING

YOUR PRINTING CHOICES. Putting a lot of ink on
paper is now just an option; a good one if there is large
prepublication demand such as advanced sales to
bookstores and/or a sale to a book club. Today, with
digital (toner) printing, there is no longer a requirement
to print 3,000 or more copies of your book "on spec".

## A. Print-on-demand (POD) Publishers.

Print-on-demand is a way of doing business not a method of printing. POD means receiving an order (and payment), manufacturing the book and then delivering the book. Most POD books are produced with digital printing but they could be produced with other methods.

Hundreds of years ago, those monks in the abbeys were POD publishers. They received an order, manufactured one book and delivered it. The only difference from today's POD publishers was that the monks hand-lettered the pages while today most POD books are manufactured on laser printers.

POD publishers supply some extra services for their relatively low price. They may take care of the cover, editing, ISBN, Library of Congress number, etc. However, the cover may be pedestrian, the editing may be minimal and the customer service may be close to non-existent. You get what you pay for.

Most POD publishers sell more books to their authors than to the public. If you take the number of books published and divide by the number of titles, you will find that less than 100 books for each title are sold.

Deal with a POD publisher when you need just a few copies of a book. For example, if you have written a family history, have a very limited budget and need up to 30 copies for your relatives, the deal offered by most POD publishers is hard to beat.

The cost per copy may be $5-10 depending upon the number of pages and the trim size. POD publishers offer an economical service when you want one to 50 copies of the book, only.

POD publishers are relatively new so their businesses are evolving. See their web sites for information on how they conduct business. For example, some require an exclusive right to use your material and some will not put your ISBN on the back cover.

See the list of POD publishers in *The Self-Publishing Manual.*

### B. Print-on-demand (POD) Printers.

POD printers, like all printers, are in the book manufacturing business and do not invest in the product.

The cost per copy may be $5-10 per copy depending upon the number of pages and the trim size.

A POD printer is a good option when a book has run its course, your inventory is exhausted and you still receive orders for a couple of copies a month. Rather than invest in inventory, you can have books made one-at-a-time as needed. Don't eat the last print run.

Some of our books are produced by LightningSource, a POD printer. See Writing Nonfiction in LARGE PRINT at http://www.amazon.com/exec/obidos/tg/detail/-/1568601166/ref=lpr_g
And
http://www.amazon.com/exec/obidos/tg/detail/-/1568601158/

This book is being produce one-at-a-time on demand for Amazon orders. But the book is being promoted by sending the regular-print edition to writing, publishing, etc. magazines. There is no need to send them the LARGE PRINT edition.

POD printers offer an economical service when you want one copy of the book, only.

POD printers do not own an exclusive on your book or supply the ISBN, They just supply a printing service.

The best known are Lightningsource (LSI), a division of Ingram the largest wholesaler, and Replica Books, part of Baker & Taylor. Another is ExactBind West, http://www.exactbindwest.com.

See the list of POD printers in *The Self-Publishing Manual*.

**C. Digital Printers--Print Quantity Needed (PQN).** Laser printing with toner.

The digital process is cost effective for quantities from 100 to 2,500 copies.

THE QUALITY of the toner-based printing is actually better. There are no light and dark pages as in ink-on-paper printing. The softcover or hardcover books look just like traditional books. Excellent, crisp color covers are usually done with the same toner process.

AUTHORS may send printed copies to agents and publishers. If an agent or publisher responds, you can entertain the offer. If not, no matter, the book is launched and you are on your way. If you send a finished book to agents and publishers, they will treat you like an author.

If you send a manuscript, you will be treated like a writer.

**PUBLISHERS** may send copies of the book to major reviewers, distributors, catalogs, specialty stores, associations, book clubs, premium prospects, foreign publishers suggesting translations and various opinion molders. After 2-3 months, you will go back to press for more. At that point, you will be able to make an educated decision on the print run based on the sales rate of the book. Therefore, PQN digital printing is the best way to start.

**HARDCOVER.** Most books are manufactured with soft covers, called "perfect binding." In offset (ink) printing, hard or "case" binding runs about $1.00 extra per book. That includes the hard covers and the dust jackets. For PQN/digital production, the cost for case binding is $2 to $4 each, depending on the page count (thickness) of the book. Case binding requires a lot of setup time. Therefore, it rarely pays to put hard covers on a short run of books.

**TIME.** Delivery for PQN digitally-printed books is normally five days from press proofs and reprints take three to four days. With your disk on file, reprints can be initiated with an email message and the books may be shipped directly to your buyer. The press proof is usually a single softcover book printed on the same paper stock you propose for the finished book.

"Once I gave approval for my new book, *Eat Stress For Breakfast*, to DeHart's Printing in Santa Clara, I had books in two days. What's great was DeHart's bid was about the same as traditional printers with only having to order half the quantity of books to get the price break. You're not investing in unneeded inventory. Since they were printed in my area, I picked

them up in my van. "I asked Dehart's if I could get some advanced copies to take to the NSA Western Workshop. He printed the copies, boxed them, and dropped them by house on his way home. When the box was opened, the books were still warm like loaves of bread. Talk about hot off the press! "Since the book was printed from a digital book file, I also have an eBook to place on my website and Internet book stores."
-- Fire "Captain Bob", http://www.eatstress.com

THE SIGNATURES of a digitally-printed book are just two pages because the print engines print cut sheets, two pages (both sides) at a time instead of 32 or 48. Now you do not have to design your book's page count in large signature increments.

MASS CUSTOMIZATION. Since the print engines are computer-driven and because your books can be printed two pages at a time, you may customize your book for your customer. If you make a premium sale to a company, it will cost just pennies to bind in a letter from the CEO or to add the company logo to the cover. You can send the insert or logo to your printer as an email attachment to save time and money.

HOW MUCH? What does it cost to manufacture a book? That is like asking how much is a car? (smile) Each book is unique. Prices will vary with the current cost of paper and labor so use the quoted numbers for comparison only.

For digital printing, the cost may be $3.50 per copy for 500 books. [Softcover (perfect bound) 144 page 5.375 x 8.375 book with black text and a four-color cover]. The per-unit price is higher than for offset printing but you are investing in a smaller number of books and the invoice will be lower.

Digital printers offer an economical service when you want a small inventory of books.

See the list of digital printers below.

**D. Offset printers.** Ink printing with plates.

Deal with an offset printer when you need 2,500 books or more.

For offset printing, the cost may be $1.25 per copy for 3,000 books. [Softcover (perfect bound) 144 page 5.375 x 8.375 book with black text and a four-color cover.] Offset printers offer an economical service when you want a larger inventory of books.

See the list off offset printers in *The Self-Publishing Manual.*

THE BEST AND SAFEST ANSWER is to print a small quantity of books. You are more likely to hear a publisher complain he or she printed too many books than too few. See http://parapub.com/sites/para/resources/newbook.cfm. And listen at http://www.jackstreet.com/jackstreet/RR.Newbookmodel.cfm. (Wait for the sound to load)

RUN THE NUMBERS/Do the math. Select the method of printing that best fits your situation. Remember that publishing involves printing and printing is a quantity game: the more your print, the lower the per-unit cost.

To help you decide on a quantity to print, total the copies you plan to send to reviewers, opinion-molders, people who sent you stories for the book and an estimate of what you might sell n the next 2-3 months.

For a list of directories and important review publications, see Document 112 (free) at http://parapub.com/sites/para/resources/allproducts.cfm. For a list of specialized review publications, see http://parapub.com/sites/para/resources/maillist.cfm Print around 500 to start, send out promotional (review, etc.) copies, sell some books and then, in a couple of months, you can make an educated decision on the size of the next print run. You need a small stock of books for promotion and sale. For inventory, printing one-at-a-time is too expensive.                                          See http://parapub.com/sites/para/information/produce.cfm

OTHER COSTS. Then there is editing, typesetting (that could be done on your computer), book cover design and other pre-press expenses. After the book is printed, it has to be promoted with book reviews, news releases and some direct email advertising. For a book like the one described above, you *used* to have to budget about $10,000 to get started. Today, with the new writing, production and promoting techniques described in *Writing Nonfiction*, you need just $2,000 to $5,000.

Your book could sell for $14.95 or $19.95 depending upon the audience. With this spread between production costs and selling price, you won't even mind giving the bookstore or other quantity-buyer a 40 percent discount.

BEWARE OF CROSS-GRAIN PRINTING. More and more printers are cheating; they are mis-manufacturing books.

Paper has a grain—just like wood. The paper in a book should have its gain oriented vertically or top to bottom. If the paper's grain is positioned horizontally, the book will have a strange feel to it. The book will not "roll" open and will want to snap shut. Your customers and book-store browsers will not know what the "problem" is but they will subconsciously feel that something is odd about your book. It will make them uncomfortable. And--you may lose the sale.

What's the problem? Printing presses are designed to print certain sizes of books. 5.5 x 8.5 is just half of 8.5 x 11 but one press should not be used to print both trim sizes. If the same press is used for both, the grain in one book will be 90 degrees off.

Some book printers have just one press for text and try to make do by printing both sizes of books. They are not competing fairly with other printers. They are not serving their publisher-customers properly.

Pick up a sheet of paper. Tear it. Now turn it 90 degrees and tear it again. The tear will be cleaner with the grain.

Pick up a book. Roll the paper in each direction with your fingers. You can usually tell which way the grain is.

When you send the request for quotations (RFQs) to printers, specify "right grain" printing. Printers know the difference. Let them know that you know the difference. Get all you are paying for.

PRODUCING FOUR-COLOR BOOKS IN SMALLER QUANTITIES just became a lot less expensive. Using your own computer, you can avoid expensive color separations and using PQN (Print Quantity Needed) technology, you can print just 100, 300, or 500 copies. See http://parapub.com/sites/para/resources/supplier.cfm

BY 2010, MORE THAN 50 PERCENT OF BOOKS SOLD WORLDWIDE WILL BE PRINTED ON DEMAND at the

point of sale in the form of library-quality paperbacks. See
http://www.longbets.org/6
and
http://www.longbets.org/bets.

PRINT ON DEMAND (POD) COSTS COMPARED. Dan Snow has polled the major POD providers and charted their quotations. See
http://www.u-publish.com/podcomp.htm

MAKING BOOKS. View a print-on-demand bookmaking machine. http://www.instabook-corporation.com/

RESURRECT OP BOOKS WITH POD. Your out-of-print books can be given new life via Print-On-Demand (POD). Unlimited Publishing will take your OP book and set it up for POD manufacture. Then the books will be manufactured one-at-a-time and only after they are sold. See
http://www.UnlimitedPublishing.com

BOOK PRINTERS. See the lists of digital and ink book printers in *The Self-Publishing Manual,* in our Special Report *Buying Book Printing* and in our Instant Report 603, *Book Printing at the Best Price.* Scroll down at http://parapub.com/sites/para/information/produce.cfm.

BUYING BOOK PRINTING answers the question we hear most, which is: How to find the best and least expensive printer for your particular book. Each printer is set up to manufacture certain kinds of books. Specialties vary depending on type of binding, book measurements, print-run, etc. This Report shows you how to make up a Request for Quotation and provides a mailing list of printers who specialize in book manufacture. A section on color printing describes how to contact local representatives of Hong Kong and other foreign printers.

This Report tells you how to decide how many books to print, how to select the appropriate binding, what to look for when checking bluelines, should you use a printing broker, how to evaluate quotations, what kind of a printing job you can expect, how to inspect the final product, and even how to resolving disputes. This Report will save you thousands of dollars in printing, binding and trucking costs. Includes an action plan, forms, sample letters and an Appendix full of resources. ISBN 1-56860-055-0, 29 pages. See http://parapub.com/sites/para/information/produce.cfm and scroll down

------------------------------------------------------------

See the "ParaSite" at http://ParaPub.com
------------------------------------------------------------

BOOK COMPONENT PRINTING. You may save money by using a different printer to print your covers, especially if you want extras such as foil-stamping, embossing, and spot UV. The trick is to ask your printer to bid separately on the text and cover printing. A comparison bid on printing the cover from a good book component printer will insure the quoted price on cover printing is a good value. These markups can be as high as 35%. Since book component printers specialize in this type of work, they offer all the extras at the lowest prices. Visit Pinnacle Press Inc. at www.pinnaclepress.com; Tel: (800) 760-0019. Email tom@pinnaclepress.com for a free sample packet and more information about book component printing.

INFOKITS. Detailed information on book writing, production, promotion and distribution.

http://parapub.com/sites/para/resources/infokit.cfm

NEED A BOOK PRINTER? See the Supplier List at
http://parapub.com/sites/para/resources/supplier.cfm

PRODUCING YOUR BOOK. Design, typesetting &
printing. Electronic and audio books.
http://parapub.com/sites/para/information/produce.cfm

NEED A BOOK MODIFIED? Want to remove a page and
insert another without disturbing the binding? For
details, contact Dunn & Co., Inc., 75 Green Street,
Clinton, MA 01510; Tel: (800) 323-0299.
http://www.booktrauma.com.

LIST OF DIGITAL PRINTERS. Check websites for
printing and other services.

aa Printing
William Ashby
6103 Johns Road, #4-5-6
Tampa, FL 33634
Tel: (813) 886-0065
Fax: (813) 884-0304
bAshby@PrintShopCentral.com
http://www.PrintShopCentral.com

Adibooks
Thomas G. Campbell
181 Industrial Avenue
Lowell, MA 01852
Tel: 978-458-2345
tcampbell@KingPrinting.com
http://www.adibooks.com

Alexander's Print Advantage
245 South 1060 West

Lindon, UT 84042
Tel: (801) 224-8666
Fax: (801) 224-0446
info@alexanders.com
http://www.Alexanders.com

BookJustBooks.com
Ron Pramschufer
51 East 42nd Street, Suite 1202
New York, NY 10017
Tel: (800) 621-2556
ron@rjcom.com
http://BooksJustBooks.com

BookMasters, Inc.
2541 Ashland Road
Mansfield, OH 44905
Tel: 800-537-6727
Fax: 419-589-4040
http://www.BookMasters.com

BookMobile.com
Nicole Baxter
2402 University Avenue
Saint Paul, MN 55114
Tel: 651-642-9241
Fax: 651-642-9153
nbaxter@bookmobile.com
http://www.BookMobile.com

Books-On-Demand
Dave Shannon, CSS Publishing
517 So. Main Street
Lima, OH 45804
Tel: 419-227-1818
http://www.CSSpub.com

BookSurge/Printorium Bookworks
A Division of Island Blue Print Ltd.
Bill Green
905 Fort Street,
Victoria, B.C. V8V 3K3
Canada
Tel: 250-385-9786
Tel: 800-661-3332
Fax: 250-385-1377
info@printoriumbookworks.com
www.printoriumbookworks.com
C&M Press
Beth Chapmon
4825 Nome Street
Denver, CO 80239
Tel: 303-375-9922
Fax: 303-375-8699
info@cmpress.com
http://www.cmpress.com/

DigiNet Printing
Guillermo "William" Perego
5723 NW 159th Street
Miami Lakes, FL 33014
Tel: (305) 825-9260
Fax: (305) 825-9294
gPerego@DigiNetPrinting.com
http://www.DigiNetPrinting.com

DeHart's Media Services Inc.
3333 Bowers Avenue
Santa Clara, CA 95054
Tel: (888) 982-4763
don@DeHarts.com
http://www.DeHarts.com

Documation LLC
Laurene Burchell
1556 International Drive
Eau Claire, WI 54701
Tel: 715-839-8899
Fax: 715-836-7411
lburchell@documation.com
http://www.documation.com

Document Technologies
Diane Gimbel
491 So. Dean St
Englewood, NJ 07631
Tel: 201-569-9600
Fax: 201-816-9191
info@xrcdti.com
http://www.xrcdti.com/

Fidlar Doubleday
Keith Reisinger
6255 Technology Avenue
Kalamazoo, MI 49001
Tel: 800- 248-0888
Tel: 248-761-9435, cell
Fax: 888-999-0655
keithr@fidlar.com
info@fidlar-doubleday.com

Gorham Printing
Kathleen Shaputis
334 Harris Road
Rochester, WA 98579
Tel: 1-800-837-0970
Fax: 1-360-273-8679
kathleens@gorhamprinting.com
http://www.gorhamprinting.com

Infinity Publishing
1094 New Dehaven Street
West Conshohocken, PA 19428
Tel: 610-520-2500
Fax: 610-519-0261
jHarnish@BuyBooksOnTheWeb.com

Morgan Printing
900 Old Koenig Lane #135
Austin, TX 78756
Tel: (512) 459-5194
Fax: (512) 451-0755
info@morganprinting.com
http://www.morganprinting.com

On-DemandPress.com
Walter Fuller
2971 Flowers Road So. #100
Atlanta, GA 30341
Tel: 770-451-4249
editor@saintbartsbooks.com
http://www.on-demandpress.com

Sir Speedy-Scottsdale
Mike Bercaw
7373 East Camelback Road
Scottsdale, AZ 85251
Tel: 480-947-7277, Ex 111
Fax: 480-946-3957
mBercaw@SirSpeedyScottsdale.com
http://www.SirSpeedy.com/scottsdale

Sir Speedy-Whittier
Tim McCarthy
7240 Greenleaf Avenue
Whittier, CA 90602
Tel: (562) 698-7513

Fax: (562) 696-0550
tim@ssWhittier.com
http://www.sswhittier.com

Starnet Media Group
P. Jeff DiPaola
50 Commerce Drive
Allendale, NJ 07401-0138
Tel: 201-760-2600
jeff@starnet-media.com
http://www.starnet-media.com

TPC Graphics
Len Metz
518 Coles Mill Road
Haddonfield, NJ 08033
Tel: 856-429-2858
Fax: 856-429-0644
TPClen-Pat@erols.com
Small run, digital, and conventional book manufacturing.
Case, soft binding.

Tri-State Litho
Kumar Persad
71 Ten Broeck Avenue
Kingston, NY 12401
Tel: (800) 836-7581
http://www.TriStateLitho.com

## PROCEDURES, BUSINESS

BUSINESS LETTERS FOR PUBLISHERS, Creative
Correspondence *Outlines* is a collection of 75 letters
drafted especially for publishers. They save time for the
older firm and enable the newer publisher to establish
company policy that conforms to current, sometimes
peculiar, publishing industry standards. Available on CD

and as a download to save you all the keyboarding. Two complete editions on one CD: MS-Word (.doc) and Adobe Acrobat (.pdf). Now you not only do not have to draft the letters, you do not have to type them. ISBN 978-0-915516-47-6.
http://parapub.com/sites/para/information/produce.cfm and scroll down.

FOR CHANGE-OF-ADDRESS NOTICES, include your old address to facilitate finding the old record. We are still getting mail for Box 4232; we switched post offices nine years ago.

INTERNATIONAL AUTHORS
--Rich Schell, JD, 847-404-2950, schell@wagneruslaw.com

If you're a publisher planning on bringing in foreign authors, consider getting a U.S. lawyer experienced in immigration to help you. How the author's compensation is set up could potentially cause serious immigration problems for him or her. As the publisher, you want to avoid the possibility of having to cancel the book tour because the author was turned away at the U.S. border.

ONLINE BACKUP SERVICES. To backup your files offsite automatically every night, see
http://www.xdrive.com
http://www.ibackup.com

WHEN ORDERING SUPPLIES by mail, telephone, fax, or online pay by credit card. If you get ripped off, you can protest the charge to your bank.

WHEN PAYING BILLS, include one of your brochures with your check. The utility companies send statement stuffers to you so why not send one back? (Note: Dan Poynter spent two college summers working in the Stub

Room [Credit Department] of the Pacific Gas & Electric Company in San Francisco. He would have seen your brochure.)

RUNNING YOUR BOOK PUBLISHING BUSINESS. Setting it up, running it and contracting.
http://parapub.com/sites/para/information/business.cfm


## PROMOTION , BOOK

BOOK PROMOTION IDEA. Hire an intern from a local college and arm the student with our step-by-step Special Reports on *Book Marketing,, Book Reviews, and News Releases*. The reports provide all the names, numbers, and direction the student will need. Interns are inexpensive and working for you will teach them valuable skills. See http://ParaPublishing.com for our Special Reports.

BOOK PROMOTION—LONG LEAD TIME. Keep marketing each week. Many clients say they are discouraged their book didn't sell well in the first four months. Replace doubt with patience for the process. There is a long lead time. Keep on promoting. Success takes many months, but once you get it, the Internet keeps it multiplied for you.
                              —Judy Cullins

"DO FIVE THINGS to promote your book each day."
                              —John Kremer

BEYOND THE BOOKSTORES by Brian Jud, book and CD special. It shows you how to sell your books to non-bookstore markets, more profitably with no returns. It contains the Marketing Planning CD-ROM™ with templates for planning and tracking sales and expenses.

See   http://www.bookmarketingworks.com/   Click   on
Beyond the Bookstore and enter the promotion code
DAN050 for a 50% savings.

HOW TO PROMOTE YOUR BUSINESS WITH
BOOKLETS. Tip Products International; 13146 Kellam
Court, Suite 133, San Diego, CA 92130. Tel: (858) 481-
0890. Tip Products helps individuals and organizations
transform their knowledge into information products for
marketing, motivating, and making money. See
http://www.tipsbooklets.com; paulette@tipsbooklets.com.
Paulette Ensign offers teleclasses on various aspects of
promoting your business with booklets. For current
schedule, see
http://www.tipsbooklets.com/teleclasses.htm;
Blog: http://www.tipsbooklets.blogspot.com

WHETHER YOU SELL OUT TO A (NY) PUBLISHER
OR PUBLISH YOURSELF, THE AUTHOR MUST DO
THE PROMOTION. What you need is a complete nuts-
and-bolts, head-to-tail, personalized promotional and
publicity plan, written tools, and easy-to-apply skills. You
can get the secrets that have earned the clients of best
selling author Raleigh Pinskey MILLIONS of dollars in
both free publicity and book sales. Get all the details at
http://www.promoteyourself.com. Tel: (480) 488-4840.
Sign up for her free "Viz-ability" tips newsletter. Raleigh
is a pro; Raleigh delivers!

CARRY YOUR BOOK WITH YOU when attending
parties and events such as leads clubs. Your book is an
attention getter and a conversation starter and
displaying it leads to sales.

"I HAD A SELF-INKING RUBBER STAMP MADE and
stamp every envelope going out with the title of my book,
the price, and the address where it may be purchased."

—Nancy Otte Waldron, author of *A Joyful Miracle*

LETTERS TO THE EDITOR. One easy way to get publicity for your books is to write letters to the editor on current events where you can make a link to your book's topic. Sign your name and the title of your book. Do not stop at one; write similar letters to local newspapers, magazines and newsletters. "Letters to the Editor" are well read and can lead to book sales, invitations for spin off articles and speaking.

PUBLICITY: AIRTIME V PRINT.
--Pam Lontos, http://www.PRPR.net

Consider the best medium for your book publicity. Radio and television work great for topics with a mass appeal, like dieting, because they reach such a huge number of people. Business topics typically work better in print.

MAKING BOOK PROMOTION PERSONAL©
The best way to show off your book's uniqueness is to make it personal. To differentiate your book from others on a similar topic is not to highlight the contents, but to spotlight your very own story. No one, no matter the subject they write on, can have your story. You are one of a kind -- at least until cloning takes over!
—Brian Feinblum, www.plannedtvarts.com, feinblumb@plannedtvarts.com

PROMOTE YOUR BOOK NATURALLY. FOR INTROVERTS AND RELUCTANT MARKETERS. Discover how to promote your book without leaving home. Learn how to reach thousands, via the Internet. Leverage what you have to get the word out. Share your book with your targeted audience—your own way. See http://www.BookCoaching.com

SHAMELESS BOOK PROMOTION. Airline pilot Lauran Paine, Jr., tapes his book cover (*Man Things*) to the cockpit door. When passengers ask, the flight attendants say: *It's the Captain's book.*

TRANSFORM YOUR MARKETING PIECES INTO DAZZLING, PERSUASIVE SALES TOOLS. Want a professional look to your book? How can you improve your promo pieces to make your marketing "pop?" What if just the right mix of "eye appeal" and "buy appeal" could help your book sales soar? Learn techniques from a pro designer, without paying high fees. Read eBooks *Turn Eye Appeal into Buy Appeal: How to easily transform your marketing pieces into dazzling, persuasive sales tools!* from Karen Saunders, MacGraphics Services. For details see http://www.BuyAppealMarketing.com

WHAT IF PUBLISHING A BOOK WAS EASIER THAN READING ONE? What if it was free? Outskirts Press is offering a free e-book from their website titled "Self-Publishing Simplified." Learn the difference between printing and POD. Discover how to get listed on Amazon for less than 55%. See
http://OutskirtsPress.com

INFOKITS. Detailed information on book writing, production, promotion and distribution.
http://parapub.com/sites/para/resources/infokit.cfm

WRITE YOUR OWN INTERVIEW ARTICLE. As you are promoting your book and questions arise about the subject matter, add the questions and answers to a growing list in your computer. When an editor calls for an article, offer the Q&A. Suggest he or she pick the questions of most interest to his or her readers. Here at Para Publishing, we have collected over 25 pages of them. See http://parapub.com/sites/para/information/business.cfm

BOOK PROMOTION MADE EASY: Event Planning, Presentation Skills & Product Marketing by Eric Gelb, MBA, CPA. Hosting events, mini seminars and workshops can provide an extremely profitable way to sell your book, other products and services. You will discover how to double or triple your profits by developing a marketing strategy, promoting more profitable events, designing your event to meet your audiences' goals, merchandising your books and other products, selling more book, products and services, making your presentation more exciting, handling the Q&A, converting your speaking engagements from free to fee and much more. Lots of inside tips and techniques. ISBN 978-1-56860-640-8, 8.5 x 11, 64 pages. Document 640.

BOOK PROMOTION WORKSHOPS consist of two days of intense training and are at Dan Poynter's home-office in Santa Barbara. For more information on investing in this event see http://parapub.com/sites/para/speaking/edutrain.cfm#doc 167
Or call 800-PARAPUB.

COMPLETE    LIST    OF    BOOK    PROMOTION DOCUMENTS
http://parapub.com/sites/para/resources/allproducts.cfm

SUCCESS STORIES. A place to list your book. http://parapub.com/sites/para/resources/successstories.cf m

MARKETING, PROMOTING & DISTRIBUTING YOUR BOOK. Wholesalers & Distributors. Book reviews, news releases, autographings, interviews, book fairs, export & foreign rights.

http://parapub.com/sites/para/information/promote.cfm

## PUBLICITY SERVICES

"HOW TO HIRE THE PERFECT PUBLICIST." This eBook by Joan Stewart shows you in step-by-step detail how to avoid the guesswork and save thousands of dollars and hours of aggravation. Learn where to find the publicist who is PERFECT for you, questions to ask, traits to look for, and how to help your publicist help you. Includes special chapters for authors and musicians. $47. http://www.publicityhound.com/hireapublicist.html

NEED SOMEONE TO TAKE YOUR BOOK TO TRADE SHOWS? See the exhibitor services on the Supplier List at http://parapub.com/sites/para/resources/supplier.cfm

"TURN-KEY PUBLICIST PACKAGE" from Michael Sedge includes: 1) development of a book website; 2) writing of one press release; 3) distribution of the release (2,800 newspapers, magazines, national wire services, and broadcast networks throughout the United States, including publishing trade magazine, and over 10,000 journalists); 4) participation in Amazon.com's sponsored results program; 5) a 60-day push to place excerpts with magazines, newspapers, and websites; 6) participation in at least one trade show; 7) and publicist services for 60 days, including working with media, editors, and journalists to place articles about books and/or get coverage for authors.

Para Publishing is proud to be the publisher of Michael Sedge's *Selling Books to the Military Market.* We have known him for many years. He is not inexpensive, but he provides great value for the cost. Contact him at msedge@thesedgegroup.com. See his work at http://www.TheSedgeGroup.com.

**PUBLISHERS WEEKLY**

*PUBLISHERS WEEKLY* WANTS INFORMATION ON YOUR FORTHCOMING BOOKS.
See http://www.publishersweekly.com/about/cfi.asp.

# Q

**QUESTIONS**

QUESTIONS AND ANSWERS ON BOOK PUBLISHING covers the basics and a lot of new material in an interview format. There are lots of small pieces of vital and encouraging publishing information that do not fit in our other Reports. This Report is fascinating and fun to read. Additionally, all authors should draft a series of questions and answers on their topic specialty to supply to editors for interview articles. This is a very cost-efficient way to get free publicity. Document 623, 20 pages. See
http://parapub.com/sites/para/information/promote.cfm#a udiobooks.

**QUOTATIONS**

QUOTATIONS SPRUCE UP YOUR BOOK BY BACKING UP YOUR POINTS. More readers will believe you if you show that someone else said it first. Most readers love to examine what others have said on the subject. For quotation sites, See
http://www.brainyquote.com and
http://www.Quotations.com.

"The average American reads one book every seven years. I just hope it's mine."
—Anonymous

# R

## RADIO & TV INTERVIEWS

GET ON THE AIR. Everyday, more than 10,200 guests appear on some 4,250 interview and talk shows across the U.S. There are shows on 988 television station. Ninety-four percent of the author-guests do not even have recognizable names.

Radio and television talk shows need interesting guests to attract listeners and viewers. Authors are interesting people; most people think that authors are experts and celebrities.

Your book will get you on, but then you must have something interesting to say that is unique, controversial, or fascinating.

Advertising on the air is expensive and people are skeptical of advertising—they tune it out. Interviews are editorial matter. People listen to editorial subjects. Interviews are more effective than advertising and they are free. Interviews can be used inexpensively to sell books.

Most of the guests booked on the shows are authors. So your book is your entrée to the airwaves.
See
http://parapublishing.com/sites/para/information/promote
.cfm and scroll down to Document 602. One of the fastest

and easiest ways to get on the air is with an ad in Radio/TV Interview Report.

RADIO INTERVIEW 101 How many are listening? --Bryan Farrish

Since radio has no visual way of showing you how many people are listening, when a guest does a radio interview by phone, he or she often doesn't know why they end up getting zero book sales (or public speaking engagements, or coaching clients, etc.) The reason is always two fold: The way they announced their contact info, and, the number of listeners that are listening. See http://www.radio-media.com/interviews/articles/intv29.htm

RECORD YOUR INTERVIEWS then convert them into an audio product. Promote as "live & unedited." See http://parapub.com/sites/para/information/promote.cfm#audiobooks.

CLIPPING SERVICE. Once you appear on TV, you may want a clipping of the show. Some services tape everything on the air and will sell you a copy.

Radio TV Reports; Tel: (323) 993-0111

Video Monitoring Services of America (VMS)
(They have offices throughout the U.S.)
330 West 42nd Street
New York, NY 10036
Tel: (212) VMS-2002
http://www.vidmon.com

National Aircheck can record any TV or radio station
http://www.National-Aircheck.com

USING RADIO & TV TO TELL THE WORLD ABOUT YOUR BOOK. Get help from Planned Television Arts, Rick Frishman; 1110 Second Avenue, New York, NY 10022; Tel: (212) 593-5820.
http://www.PlannedTVArts.com; frishmanr@plannedtvarts.com.

Free Radio Airtime, Alex Carroll; 924 Chapala Street, #D, Santa Barbara, CA 93101.
Tel: (877) 733-3888; http://www.RadioPublicity.com; alex@radiopublicity.com. Top radio station database & booking secrets from veteran of 1,000+ interviews.

Bradley Communications, Bill Harrison, 135 East Plumstead Avenue, #215, Lansdowne, PA 19050. Tel: (800) 553-8002. Getting on radio and TV through the *Radio-TV Interview Report.*

SPIN BREAKING NEWS. Initially, he focused his attention on his book. Then Captain Bob realized, "It's not the book, stupid! It's the many ways you can pitch your material to hook the producer into wanting to put you on the air. Like many other relationship authors, I was trying to get interviews for Valentine's Day. The press release went out with 'Get Everything You Want from the Opposite Sex.' We weren't getting much response. Then the Clinton-Monica story broke. We immediately changed the news release to: 'President Clinton's Situation. Could it Happen to You?" Immediate bookings." Capitalize on the breaking news.
—Fire "Captain Bob" http://www.eatstress.com

HOW I GOT ON THE BARBARA WALTERS SHOW. An inspiring story from (Fire) Captain Bob. See http://www.eatstress.com/tips.htm.

MEDIA COACHING. There are many ways to get on radio and TV. See
http://parapub.com/sites/para/information/promote.cfm.
However, what do you do once you get there? How do you take maximum advantage of the media opportunity? Joel Roberts is a dynamic, caring, sharing coach who can help turn you into a media star. Contact him at joelroberts@mac.com or (310) 286-0631.

NEED RADIO AND TV COACHING? See the Supplier List at
http://parapub.com/sites/para/resources/supplier.cfm

SBTV CAN PROMOTE AUTHORS ON THE AUTHORS CHANNEL. If you have a book on entrepreneurism or small business, go to their website at
http://www.sbtv.com.

WANT TO SUGGEST A SHOW TO OPRAH? You will have a better chance of getting on if you propose a program that includes a controversial topic. Include yourself, a supporter, and a detractor. See Oprah's website at http://www.oprah.com,
http://www.oprah.com/email/reach/email_showideas.jhtml

17 SECRETS TO SUCCESSFUL RADIO/TV PUBLICITY, AND A REPORT, *39 Ways to Sell Your Book through Radio-TV Publicity*. Call Radio-TV Interview Report at (800) 989-1400. Free. RTIR is the fastest, easiest and probably the least expensive way to get radio and TV exposure.

NEED SOMEONE TO GET YOU ON RADIO AND TV? See the Supplier List at
http://parapub.com/sites/para/resources/supplier.cfm

## REFERENCE SITES

ACRONYMS. According to author, Derrick Hayes, POYNTER stands for "Publish One of Your New Titles to Educate Readers." Derrick has a whole book of these "Derricknyms," titled *Derricknyms from A to Z— Acronyms with a touch of Derrick where words are motivational messages.* DerrickHayes@aol.com; http://www.derrickhayes.com

CONVERT ANY NUMBERS.
See http://www.megaconverter.com/mega2/.
Bookmark this site.

GET IMPORTANT REFERENCE BOOKS FOR MUCH, MUCH LESS. Libraries often replace reference materials, and donate them to the Friends to sell at their Used Book Sales. It's a great opportunity to stock up on office reference materials. I have purchased Literary Market Place (retails around $300), Gale Directories, business books, lists of associations, lists of newsletters, Style Manuals, Writers' Market, computer manuals, business magazines, etc., and never paid more than a few dollars for any of them! A lot of book sales are held in the summer and fall, so it's a great time to stock the office for pennies on the dollar. Got kids? Bring them along— they'll leave with armloads of books without breaking the piggy bank. Book Sale Finder is a free listing of the dates, locations, and times of the sales. Visit often. It's updated several times a week. And if you're a used book aficionado, join personalized Sale Mail: You tell Book Sale Finder how far you're willing to travel, and you'll get email telling you when there are sales in your area—it's all free. Book Sale Finder: The Online Guide to Used Book Events at http://www.BookSaleFinder.com.

LEARN ABOUT THE ORGANIZATION OR INDUSTRY you are writing about.
http://www.corporateinformation.com.

LIVE IN A CITY AND WANT TO KNOW THE TRAFFIC SITUATION? Get real-time traffic reports at http://www.Traffic.com

MEDIA DIRECTORIES are often out of date by the time the ink is dry or the CD-ROM is burned. Before you write a pitch letter to a media contact, it's best to call to make sure he or she still works there.
—Joan Stewart, The Publicity Hound
http://www.PublicityHound.com

NEED A SPECIALIZED DICTIONARY? Need to check unique aviation, medicine, military, etc. words? See these dictionaries:
http://www.alphadictionary.com
http://www.yourdictionary.com

QUICK ONLINE DICTIONARY: GOOGLE. Type define:word (without spaces) and Google will define the word.

PUBLISHER CONTACT LIST. See the Publishing Trends website. Packed with industry, phone, and email addresses, now downloadable in PDF. Go to http://www.publishingtrends.com

REFERENCE LIBRARIES. Visit the Virtual Library at http://www.vlib.org. For world and local news and historical events, go to http://www.refdesk.com.

SEARCHING THE WEB AND BEYOND. A9.com remembers your information so you don't have to. You

can store and organize your bookmarks. It recommends new sites and favorite old sites specifically for you to visit. With the A9 Toolbar installed, your web browsing history will be saved so you can search through your whole history (and clear items you don't want kept). See http://a9.com
—Jim Zinger, http://www.JimZinger.com

THE FEDERAL TRADE COMMISSION (FTC), regulator of sales by telephone, mail, fax, email, etc., has a website at http://www.ftc.gov.

THE ORIGIN OF SMILEYS REVEALED.
http://www.newbie.net/SmileyFAQ/Fahlman.html

THE SMALL BUSINESS RESOURCE GUIDE, Publication 3207, is free from the U.S. Internal Revenue Service. It is a CD-ROM with business tax forms, publications, information on business plans, record keeping, financing and retirement plans and tutorials, updates, and resource lists. You can get one free copy by calling (800) 829-3676.

THE WEB ACRONYM AND ABBREVIATION SERVER translates acronyms.
http://www.ucc.ie/cgi-bin/acronym/

WANT TO RESEARCH A TRADEMARK? See http://www.uspto.gov/main/trademarks.htm.

WHAT TIME IS IT? Just click on a city and get the time. See
http://www.timeanddate.com/worldclock/
http://www.timezoneconverter.com
Also see http://www.worldtimeserver.com.
(Turn off popup blocker)
For the official U.S. time, see http://www.time.gov.

## RESOURCES AND RESEARCH LINKS
http://parapub.com/sites/para/resources/researchlinks.cfm

WORDS. Anagrams, crossword helpers, pig Latin, word morph, crypto crackers and more. See
http://www.wordplays.com/p/index

WORDTRIPPERS: *A Quick Guide to Using Words that Trip You Up* by Barbara McNichol. This delightful pamphlet distinguishes between words such as Among & Between, Appear & Seem, Hanged & Hung, Irritate, & Aggravate, and many more. If you work with words, you need this guide. Check out her website at http://www.barbaramcnichol.com and she will mail it to you. editor@barbaramcnichol.com

## RELIGIOUS BOOKS

RELIGIOUS BOOKS. In the final decade of the 20th century there was a sharp increase in the market for religious books. The interest in the new millennium may have been one cause of this increase. But the interest continues because of the rising levels of education, fading commitments to tradition, sectarian religion, and a hunger for the spiritual.

Although traditional religious titles are still being published and have a vast audience, books that reflect a contemporary search for God or a personal spirituality are taking up more shelf space in American bookstores. Books that reflect religious concerns or quests are constantly appearing on the bestseller lists.

People feel freer than ever before to investigate many religious expressions and to adopt ideas and practices for a range of faiths. It is often easier to take religious questions to the bookstore than to seek out the local priest, rabbi, or minister. The bookstore is the place many carry out their quest. Here, people can discover the potentially life-changing power of a book.

FOR A LIST OF DISTRIBUTORS OF RELIGIOUS BOOKS, see our Instant Report Locating the Right Distributor, Document 605. See http://parapublishing.com/sites/para/information/promote .cfm and scroll down.

FOR A LIST OF 504 RELIGIOUS MAGAZINES, newsletters and other religion-industry contacts, see http://parapub.com/sites/para/resources/maillist.cfm .

RELIGIOUS BOOKS; Resources for Writing, Producing and Promoting theological books. Lists the information sources you need to successfully publish and promote religious books. Document 618, 4 pages. See http://parapublishing.com/sites/para/information/promote .cfm and scroll down.

## REMAINDERS

BUYING AND SELLING REMAINDERS. See http://www.skuflow.com/ssl/myremainders/

WANT TO DUMP EXCESS INVENTORY? See PMA's Remainder Book Fair at http://www.pma-online.org.

BEYOND REMAINDERS describes creative inventory reduction. When sales of a book drop off, it is time to move out the balance, before they get too old, to make room for new books. There are many easy ways to reduce inventory besides remaindering and they bring in more money. An action plan, sample letters, addresses, and resources are included. Document 633, 11 pages. See http://parapub.com/sites/para/information/business.cfm and scroll down.

## REPRINTS & REVISED EDITIONS

AS A PUBLISHER, YOU HAVE THE AUTHORITY to call any reprinting a "revision." When going back to press, you should always make corrections, add updates, assign a new ISBN, and a new bar code. Then your book will be treated as *frontlist*, a new book, by the trade.

WRITE IT ONCE—SELL IT FOREVER, How to Update Your Books. It is a lot easier to sell a revised edition of the same book than it is to write a new one. Updating a book can be quick and easy if you have a plan. This *Instant Report* provides that plan. Set up your system now. Document 619, 5 pages. See http://parapub.com/sites/para/information/writing.cfm. Scroll down.

## RESEARCH

RESEARCHING YOUR TOPIC. How can you get accurate sales figures for other published books? You really can't. Traditionally, publishers do not publish sales figures. In fact, they boast of the number of books "in print" (and waiting to be sold). The "In-Print" figure shows their commitment to the book—and often the number is inflated. Most books are printed in quantities of 5,000.

Whether you are planning to find an agent and sell out to a publisher or publish yourself, you need numbers. You, or the publisher, need the reassurance of a definable, reachable market. Do this research *before* you write the book.

Nielsen's BookScan tries to count book sales. See http://www.BookScan.com/. They operate the first continuous retail sales monitoring service for books, with purchase information representing sales through a majority of the major retailers each week. In a typical week, sales of more than 300,000 different titles are collected, coded and analyzed, producing market information for retailers, publishers and the media. But they cover only 80% of the stores—just 4,500 book retailers and many more books are sold outside these bookstores. You must subscribe to the BookScan service to get the numbers you seek.

In order to qualify your project, you must get an idea of the numbers of prospective buyer/readers for it. You can't get absolute figures but you can get comparative numbers. Here are the steps.

A. BOOKSTORES. Visit a couple of bookstores with a notepad. Large stores have a wider selection than small stores. Visit the right neighborhood. For example, downtown stores will have a greater selection of business books while stores in the suburbs will have more books on parenting and relationships. Some stores have special (enlarged) departments for some genres.

Look on that shelf where your book will be. Remember that your book will be compared (shopped) with the books adjacent to it. Look at each book. Think: if someone were to see this book, would they also be interested in my book? Chart the (comparative) books on your pad. Write down the title, subtitle, author, trim size, page count, copyright date, edition, cover type ISBN and price.

B. ONLINE STORE. Log on to a store such as Amazon.com. Search for your category of book and set the list for Publication-Date order. Now you will see all of the books in your field from the brand new ones and going back 20 years. Chart the books that are close to your project.

You will find a lot of the same books you found in the stores but the ones in the stores are either newer or selling better; Amazon has space for virtually every book. At Amazon, the readers evaluate the books. Write down how many stars each book is averaging. Amazon also provides the sales ranks; they tell you how the books are selling against each other. Write down the numbers.

For historical Amazon sales data, go to
http://www.titlez.com/welcome.aspx

C. INGRAM. Call the computer at Ingram, 615-213-6803. Follow the voice prompts and punch in the ISBN (found on the back) of any book. The recorded voice will tell you how many books are in each warehouse, what the weekly sales rate is, how many were sold last year and how many were sold, so far, this year. Ingram moves some 55% of the books in the U.S.; these are not absolute sales figures, they are comparative figures.

D. MAGAZINES. How many periodicals serve the group you want to sell to? See
http://parapub.com/sites/para/resources/maillist.cfm
If there are a lot of magazines, there must be a lot of potential buyers for your book. Go to the websites of each magazine and look for the circulation figures. People who subscribe to magazines, do so voluntarily and vote (subscribe) with their money.

BTW, you will send review copies to many of theses magazines and newsletters. Reviews are the least expensive and most effective promotion you can do for your book. Bookmark the sites.

E. ASSOCIATIONS. How many clubs and associations have your potential buyers joined? What is the size of the membership of each organization? Make online searches and see directories such as the Encyclopedia of Associations, http://library.dialog.com/bluesheets/html/bl0114.html and http://www.MarketingSource.com/Associations/

F. STORES. What stores do your potential buyers frequent? For numbers of specialty stores and chain stores, see http://www.vendorpro.com/stores.htm

You will probably sell more of your books through specialty stores than bookstores. See http://parapub.com/sites/para/information/promote.cfm

For other industry numbers, see http://www.Ranks.com

G. EVENTS. Where do your potential buyers voluntarily come together because they have a like interest? What events do they attend? How many are there regionally and nationally? How many people attend? Relevant conventions and other events are good places to sell individual books and to make new dealers.

H. CATALOGS. More than 7,000 catalogs are published in the U.S.; 11.8 billion are mailed each year. See the catalog directories at your public library and http://www.catalogs.google.com/. You are not interested in "book" catalogs, you want specialty catalogs. For example, match a skydiving book with a parachute catalog. How many catalogs are there in your field? How many copies do they distribute? Record the numbers. You will want to submit your book to these catalogs. See Document 625, Selling Books to Catalogs at http://parapub.com/sites/para/resources/allproducts.cfm

I. GOOGLE PRINT. You can research the texts of many new books through Google's new program. For information, see http://www.print.google.com/

Total up all these numbers. Now you should have a good feel for what has been published in your area and what hasn't been done, what is selling and what is not selling, how much you can charge for your book, etc.

See the Statistics Bank. Fascinating numbers on book publishing.
http://parapub.com/sites/para/resources/statistics.cfm

Whether you are selling out to a publisher or publishing yourself, you need numbers. Agents and publishers want figures; you need them too. If you are selling out, put these numbers in your proposal, your agent will think you are a marketing genius.

AREA CODES: http://www.555-1212.com/geo.isp

SCIENCE WEBSITE brings together many U.S. Government agency websites into one portal. http://www.science.gov.

COMPREHENSIVE SEARCH TOOL. When you need facts, theories, maps, dictionaries, translations try http://www.itools.com/research-it/. Bookmark this site.

CUSTOM RESEARCH SERVICES. Great site for fiction and nonfiction writers, speechwriters, editors, and others. Expert searching of the world's most comprehensive online databases, including those from Dialog, Nexis, Datastar, IAC, ProQuest, Dow Jones, Thomson, and Wilson.
http://www.researchforwriters.com

FREE RESEARCH SERVICES. Invaluable when writing or promoting a book. Markus Allen recommends these two sites:
http://www.tracerlock.com
http://alerts.yahoo.com

GLOSSARY OF BOOK TRADE TERMINOLOGY. See http://www.publishers.org.uk/paweb/paweb.nsf/pubframe ?open

GOVERNMENT REPORTS. The United States government stocks a treasure trove of geographic and demographic data—yours FREE for the asking. Check out http://www.govspot.com. Many thanks for this resource from Markus Allen, the mailing guru. See http://www.markusallen.com.

17,000 FEDERAL, STATE, AND LOCAL GOVERNMENT INFORMATION SITES. See
http://www.govengine.com
-- jimzinger@jimzinger.com

HOW DOES YOUR WEBSITE RANK for traffic, speed, and links? See
http://www.alexa.com.

HOW THINGS WORK. Great resource site. See
http://www.howstuffworks.com.

INTERACTIVE CENSUS MAPS. See
http://barbera.caliper.com/maptitude/census2000maps/ma
p.asp

INVESTIGATE PUBLIC RECORDS. Check out this site:
http://www.knowx.com.

LATIN-ENGLISH Cross References
http://www.wordsources.info

LOG TO ALTA VISTA (http://www.altavista.com) and
search for graphics or images. Many thanks to Jim Zinger
for this tip.

NEWSPAPER RESOURCE. Both established newspapers
and alternative newspapers from around the world.
Search alphabetically by newspaper name by continent.
Links are to the newspaper sites; you then search the
individual sites for materials relevant to your interests.
See http://www.onlinenewspapers.com. —Jim Zinger

ONLINE SEARCH TOOL. Search Word Pro is an online
search tool that is designed to search in search engines,
blogs, invisible Web resources, government search
engines, magazines, and news search engines, and sites
in a new way. See
http://www.econtentmag.com/NewsLetters/NewsletterRea
der.aspx?NewsletterID=245#10 —Paul Krupin

POPULAR NEW WORDS or new uses are
http://www.wordspy.com and
http://www.verbatimmag.com.

RESEARCH: FORECASTING THE FUTURE. See:
http://www.wfs.org
http://www.iftf.org
http://www.trendtalk.com/

RESEARCH RESOURCE. Whether you cover politics or sports, medicine or pets, the workplace or the environment, SourceNet can help you find the information you need, when you need it. Use SourceNet to post a query to find quotations, opinions, product news, or general information on broad or niche topics quickly. All queries are completely anonymous; your personal contact information is never sent to PR people. See MediaMap's Tools for Journalists at
http://sourcenet.mediamap.com.

RESEARCH SITES. Global Internet user trends: http://StatMarket.com. Forecasts and analyses of emerging technologies: http://idc.com. —Judy Byers

RESEARCH TOOL. GOOGLISM: Who, what, when, and where. See
http://www.googlism.com/about.htm

RESEARCH TREASURE TROVE. All types of news: business, technology, sports, health. Get information on other topics of interest. Go to www.excite.com. Enter the key words. The site will collect articles for you on that subject. It may also be used as a clipping service.

DICTIONARY. See
http://dictionary.reference.com/

REVERSE DICTIONARY. See
http://www.wordtree.com
http://www.onelook.com/reverse-dictionary.shtml

THESAURUS. See
http://www.visualthesaurus.com/index.jsp

THE ALEX CATALOGUE OF ELECTRONIC TEXTS is a collection of public domain documents from American and English literature as well as Western philosophy. See http://www.infomotions.com/alex.

WHO IS SELLING YOUR BOOK? Is it at Wal-Mart, Powells and/or Half.com? For a list, see http://www.bookhq.com and http://www.fetchbook.info.

YAHOO'S IMAGE SEARCH indexes over 630 million images and is worth a look. http://images.search.yahoo.com/info/image_whatsnew.ht ml –Jim Zinger, www.jimzinger.com

ZIP CODES. Click on a map to find any zip code. http://maps.huge.info/zip.htm

FOR TIME ANYWHERE IN THE WORLD and international country/city/phone codes: http://www.gchart.com

RESEARCH. HERE ARE SOME GREAT WEB SITES YOU WILL FIND USEFUL
--Rick Frishman, Planned TV Arts, frishmanr@plannedtvarts.com, www.plannedtvarts.com

Local PRSA Chapters: www.prsa.org
The Institute for PR: www.instituteforpr.com
American Society of Association Executives: www.asaenet.org
International Association of Business Communicators: www.iabc.com
National Investor Relations Institute (NIRI): www.niri.org
Trade Publications/Information
PR Reporter: www.prpublishing.com

The Ragan Report: www.ragan.com
PR Week: www.prweekus.com
PR News:
www.prandmarketing.com/cgi/catalog/info?PRN
O'Dwyer's: www.odwyerpr.com
Corporate Philanthropy Report: www.grantscape.com

SEARCH TOOLS OR SEARCH SITES
Lexis Nexis: www.lexisnexis.com
LuceOnline: www.luceonline.com
About.com: www.publicrelations.about.com
Hoover's Online: www.hoovers.com
IPO Central: www.ipocentral.com
Edgar Online: www.edgar-online.com
InfoSeek: www.infoseek.com

WIRE SERVICES
US Newswire: www.usnewswire.com
Feature Photo Service: www.featurephoto.com
PRNewswire: www.prnewswire.com
Business Wire: www.businesswire.com
Reuters: www.reuters.com

MEDIA MONITORING
Deja News: www.dejanews.com
Inquisit: www.inquisit.com

ADDITIONAL WEB SITES
PR Counselors Academy: www.prsa-counselors.org
American Marketing Association: www.ama.org
Business Marketing Association: www.marketing.org
The Association for Women in Communication:
www.WOMCOM.org
Council of Public Relations Firms: www.prfirms.org
The Conference Board: www.conference-board.org

STUFF YOU REALLY USE:
Ticketmaster: www.ticketmaster.com
TeeMaster: www.teemaster.com
MapQuest: www.mapquest.com


## RETURNS, BOOK

BOOK RETURNS are one the most frustrating aspects of
the book industry for any publisher. Though the majority
of returns are overstock returns, damaged returns are
also a big part of this problem. If you do your own
fulfillment, inspect each book carefully and don't ship
product with dents or scratches on the cover, a bent
spine, or glue residue. They will come back to you. If your
book is case bound, extra dust jackets are a worthwhile
investment if re-jacketing them means the difference
between "saleable" and "un-saleable" product. Thanks to
Clint Greenleaf, CEO of Greenleaf Book Group, LP at
www.greenleafbookgroup.com.

BEYOND REMAINDERS describes creative inventory
reduction. When sales of a book drop off, it is time to
move out the balance, before they get too old, to make
room for new books. There are many easy ways to reduce
inventory besides remaindering and they bring in more
money. An action plan, sample letters, addresses, and
resources are included. Document 633, 11 pages. See
http://parapub.com/sites/para/information/business.cfm
and scroll down.

RECYCLING RETURNS
--Clint Greenleaf, CEO of Greenleaf Book Group, LP
www.greenleafbookgroup.com or 512-891-6100

Returns are one the most frustrating aspects of the book
industry for any publisher. Though the majority of

returns are overstock returns, damaged returns are also a big part of this problem. If you do your own fulfillment, inspect each book carefully and don't ship product with dents or scratches on the cover, a bent spine, or glue residue. They will come back to you. If your book is case bound, extra dust jackets are a worthwhile investment if re-jacketing them means the difference between "saleable" and "un-saleable" product.

FORM, Book Return Authorization. An example of the verbiage we use. See Document 134 at http://parapub.com/sites/para/resources/allproducts.cfm

## REVIEWS, REVIEWERS, SOURCES

ARTICLE ON THE IMPORTANCE OF REVIEWS. See Document 126 at http://parapub.com/sites/para/resources/allproducts.cfm

EDITORIAL COPY V ADVERTISING COPY. On the average, people spend seven minutes with their magazines. Obviously, they see very few of the ads. Of those ads they see, they read very few. Of those ads they read, they believe very few. Of those ads they believe, they act on very few. People are skeptical of advertisements. On the other hand, readers believe editorial copy. Now ask yourself: How much advertising space can you buy for $900? Not much—and it will not sell many books anyway. So, why not send out review copies that will result in editorial copy that people will believe?

BOOK REVIEWS shows you in detail how to take advantage of the free publicity available to books from the pre-publication galleys to a continuing review program. Book reviews are your least expensive and most effective form of book promotion. Reviews are not hard to get if you follow the unwritten (until now) rules. This Report provides paint-by-the-numbers instructions for making galleys and provides a detailed action plan about how to set up a review program so your books will be reviewed again and again. It covers pre-publication reviews, early reviews, retail reviews, and continuing reviews with examples of the packages for each. The Report even tells you what to do with the reviews after you receive them. Complete with lists of major reviewers and sources for the rest. Examples and resources. See Document 116. ISBN 1-56860-032-1, 35 pages. See http://parapublishing.com/sites/para/information/promote .cfm#bkrev. Scroll down.

DON'T LIMIT YOUR PITCH to the top twenty publications. Hundreds of magazines are out there. If someone sees your name in a trade publication, your quotation in the newspaper, your article in a small magazine, and finally your interview in Entrepreneur, then your name will jump off the page at them and will be burned into their memory.

BOOK REVIEW SOURCES. Casey Hill. http://www.newpages.com/NPGuides/reviews.htm

FOLLOW UP IMPROVES RESULTS. When you send a review copy of your book or a news release to a periodical, it never hurts to follow up with a telephone call. There is nothing wrong with calling—just do not make a counter-productive pest of yourself. Simply ask if the book has been received. If not, get a name and send another—and then call again. Reviewers know that many books get ripped off in the mailroom (and sold to a used-book store) and never get upstairs to them.

LIST OF BOOK REVIEWERS. Check the Categories for types of books wanted. Most are for Romance fiction. See http://www.rio-reviewers.com/membership/rio-members.html.

GALLEY COVER LAYOUT FORM. Paint by the number outline. See Document 149 at http://parapub.com/sites/para/resources/allproducts.cfm

MORE INFORMATION on books reviews, author interviews and literary news at the following website: http://www.compulsivereader.com

PAID BOOK REVIEWS? Should you pay for a review? Hear the opinions of various book-industry leaders on Dan Poynter's Publishing Poynters Radio. http://www.jackstreet.com/jackstreet/KPNT.E2.cfm (Takes a while to load)

PROMOTION IS LESS EXPENSIVE AND MORE SUCCESSFUL when you use book reviews, news releases and, if appropriate to your book, a limited amount of highly-targeted direct email advertising.

Book reviews are *editorial copy* that is much less expensive and far more credible than space advertising. For most nonfiction books, there are over 500 appropriate magazines, newsletters, and newspapers columns that should receive review packages.

For lists of appropriate media, visit http://www.parapublishing.com/sites/para/resources/maillist.cfm. To find out how good Para Publishing's lists are, call a recent client: Godfrey Harris at Harris/Ragan Management Group: (310) 278-8037.

REVIEW COPIES, AN EXCELLENT PROMOTION INVESTMENT. Sending out books for review is the most effective and one of the least expensive things you can do for your book. Para Publishing maintains mailing lists for more than 90 types of magazines, newsletters and newspaper columns. Just a few are parenting, seniors, business, horses, banking, and advertising. See http://www.parapublishing.com/sites/para/resources/maill ist.cfm.

DON'T OVERLOK THE SMALLER PERIODICALS
—Pam Lontos, http://www.PRPR.net

WHERE TO SEND BOOKS FOR REVIEW. Before you send your new book off to specialized magazines and newsletters, send them to the following special reviewers and other important contacts. Build your review foundation.

In anticipation of your new book coming off the press, address shipping bags to those places listed below and stuff them, as appropriate, with cover letter, review slip, photocopied Advance Book Information form, and a 4" x 6" or larger black-and-white photograph of the book's cover. Include brochures, copies of early reviews and other materials to convince reviewers that the book has been accepted by others. Do not skimp here. Then when the truck arrives from the printer, stuff the books into the bags and ship them off.

Note what is said about each of the addressees in Document 112, because some may not be appropriate to your book. If yours is an adult scientific text, do not bother to send it to the *Horn Book* magazine, which reviews children's books.

See Send Finished Books in Document 112, *Poynter's Secret List of Book Promotion Contacts* at http://www.parapublishing.com/sites/para/resources/allpr oducts.cfm. Scroll on down.

Time is of the essence. These early review copies must be sent out as soon as the truck arrives from the printer. Reviewers like new books. Books are copyright dated so it is easy to tell when they are not new. Equally important, most of your initial sales will come from these reviews. So if you do not get moving with your review copy program, that inventory will not move out. Meanwhile, the dated books are getting older every day.

Once you have completed the above, follow the instructions in Dan Poynter's Special Reports *Book Marketing and Book Reviews*. Both reports provide step-by-step instructions with check-off lists to make sure you cover all the bases and that you do so in the right order.

IS IT EVER TOO LATE TO SEND OUT REVIEW COPIES? The book trade is only interested in new books. Special-interest magazines are concerned about the value of the (nonfiction) information. Of course, it is best to send out review copies as soon as the books arrive from the printer, but it is never too late if the book is not out of date. For a list of special-interest magazines, see http://parapub.com/sites/para/resources/maillist.cfm

REVIEW MEDIA STATISTICS. Want to know how many books the periodicals review each year? See http://www.BookWire.com/bookwire.

THE PRE-PUBLICATION REVIEWERS. Where to send the galleys.
1. Publishers Weekly
2. Library Journal

3. ALA Booklist
4. Choice magazine
5. Foreword Magazine
6. Kirkus Reviews
7. NY Times Book Review
8. LA Times Magazine
9. School Library Journal
10. Quality Books (library distributor)
11. Major & matching book clubs

GALLEYS AND PUB DATES, see Document 608, *Your Publication Date.*
http://parapublishing.com/sites/para/information/promote.cfm and scroll down.

PROMOTION TIP: To get pre-publication reviewers to pay attention to your galleys, don't use shipping bags. Pack the books in Nieman-Marcus boxes.
--Charlotte Degregorio of Portland, Oregon.

DO NOT MAIL REVIEW COPIES between November 15 and December 27. Some could wind up as holiday gifts—and never be reviewed. Plan the mail drop for December 31.

IS IT EVER TOO LATE TO SEND OUT REVIEW COPIES? The book trade is only interested in new books. Special interest magazines are concerned on the value of the (nonfiction) information. Of course, it is best to send out review copies as soon as the books arrive from the printer, but it is never too late as long as the book is not out of date. For a list of special interest magazines, see http://parapub.com/sites/para/resources/maillist.cfm

RUBBER STAMP YOUR REVIEW COPIES. They will still be sold but they won't be returned to you by a bookstore for a refund.

REVIEW COPY RUBBER STAMPING seen on *Handcuff Blues* from Goofy Foot Press:

## WOW! A Review Copy!

SEND REVIEW COPIES TO GAY NEWSPAPERS. Many gay people have high disposable incomes. They are able to attend the theater often, take trips, and buy a lot of CDs and books. Most of the gay publications review books on all subjects and are likely to review your books since they have been somewhat ignored by mainstream publishers. See "The Harris Guide 2001." (ISBN: 0970127405). --Peter Smith.

BOOKS ON CONTEMPORARY SPIRITUALITY WANTED FOR REVIEW. Send to Fearless Books, 2342 Shattuck Ave. #506, Berkeley, CA 94704, (800) 480-2776. http://www.fearlessbooks.com; info@fearlessbooks.com

BOOKVIEW.COM welcomes books for review. Send only published books, not galleys or proofs. Alan Caruba, Editor, Bookviews.com, 28 West Third Street. # 1321, South Orange, NJ 07079. See http://www.bookviews.com.

# S

## SALES TAXES

CALIFORNIA DOES NOT COLLECT SALES TAXES on shipping supplies, on printing delivered to a mailing house, or on mailing-list rental. Presumably, this keeps business in the state and promotes exports. Notify your carton supplier and brochure printer not to charge you sales tax.

## SCAMS

READ BOOKS FOR FUN AND PROFIT? The get-rich-quick people are at it again. In direct mail and space ads, they claim you can make a lot of money reading manuscripts for busy publishers. Send them money and you get a list of publishers with directions on how to write to them. Thousands of unsuspecting, well-meaning people have approached hundreds of publishers offering their services. Usually the publishers try to answer the letters and explain why they do not need or want outside help. Then, eventually, the burden becomes too great and the publishers have to ignore the letters. Reading for profit is not the only scam. The unwary are sending money for "Watch Television for Pay," "Read Classified Ads for Pay," and many more.

## SCANNERS

GETTING THE MOST FROM YOUR SCANNER. Did you know that if you rotate an image after scanning, you can lose detail? See
http://www.homeandoffice.hp.com/hho/us/eng/how_to_scan.html

## SCREENWRITING

SCREENWRITING: Fiction (theatricals) & Nonfiction (documentaries) by Gail Kearns is jammed with tips, ideas and resources on writing screenplays from Movies-of-the-Week to sitcoms. She also tells you how to protect your work. Document 638, 8 pages. See
http://parapub.com/sites/para/information/writing.cfm
and scroll down.

## SELF-PUBLISHING

AUTHORS CAN LEARN FROM ACTORS. Why did Stephen King elect to sell eBook installments of "The Plant" from his own website? Why are more and more famous authors choosing alternative publishing paths like self-publishing and POD? For the same reason movie actors began working for multiple studios in the 1940s and 50s. More control, more creativity, more money.

Do you think actors today would be making $20 million a movie if the studios were still in charge? Only when they became free agents did their autonomy soar. Their paychecks followed suit.

Soon thereafter the independent film industry was born, leading the way for a similar revolution in the 1990s with the dawn of independent music.

The publishing industry is in the middle of this change now. Viva la revolution. Read more in "Self-Publishing Simplified" available at
http://outskirtspress.com/publishing
—Brent Sampson, http://outskirtspress.com

SHOULD YOU SELF-PUBLISH? For a self-paced quiz, see http://www.happilypublished.com/self.html.

DOES SELF-PUBLISHING WORK? It worked for John Grisham, Richard Nixon and Stephen King. See Document 155 at
http://parapub.com/sites/para/resources/allproducts.cfm
and see
http://parapub.com/sites/para/resources/success_list.cfm

EVERYTHING YOU SHOULD KNOW ABOUT
PUBLISHING, PUBLICITY & BUILDING a PLATFORM
by Arielle Ford is a step-by-step resource guide that is an
insider's blueprint to jump start your career as an author
and publisher.

The 5-CD, 180 page course reveals every secret and
strategy she's used for the past fifteen years including her
contacts at Oprah, samples of press releases, pitch
letters, bio's and documentation she sends to the media.
Besides taking these authors careers to undreamed of
heights, including getting them on Oprah, Good Morning
America and countless other programs, Arielle has
written six books herself. She is both an author and a
publicist.

See   http://www.everythingyoushouldknow.com/dp/   and
note the discount. Be sure to sign up for Arielle's free
"Bestseller Strategies" newsletter too. There's a sign-up
page right on the website.

SELF-PUBLISHING FOR THE CLUELESS. Mike
Rounds,  a self-published author, explains how to do the
following on his CD:

-Write a book in 30 days or less
-Write tips booklets in one day
-Create audio CD's in two weeks
-Convert PowerPoint™ to high-profit products
-Create e-Books for under $1.00 each

The CD contains a complete information manual that
includes examples and resources for bar codes, typing and
transcription services, cover designs, and low cost
printing sources. See
 http://www.cluelessmike.com/self_publishing.htm.

SELF-PUBLISHING GARNERS RESPECT. Traditionally, when a publishing CEO or other prominent
individual wrote a memoir, he or she would seek another
publisher to release it so that the book would not appear
to be a vanity work. Times have changed. Self-publishing
has become so recognized and legitimate that the vanity
stigma has nearly disappeared. For a list of self-published
books that rocketed to the tops of the charts, see
http://parapublishing.com/sites/para/information/access.cf
m?isbn=Document%20155&qty=1&isdl=1

SELF-PUBLISHING TODAY: Tapping Into the
Economics of Abundance. See
http://www.bob-baker.com/qt/abundance.html

SMALLER AND NEWER NONFICTION BOOK
PUBLISHERS HAVE SEVERAL ADVANTAGES over
the large (New York) publishers: As authors and
publishers, we are closer to our subject matter (we know
good material); as participants in our topic, we are closer
to our customers (we know how to find them). We can get
to press sooner so our material is fresher. We revise our
books with each printing so our material is always
current. We are more nimble and can quickly change with
the market. In nonfiction book publishing, being small is
an advantage—an unfair advantage.

**SELLING BOOKS**

BOOKSHELF. Selling Books From Other Publishers
shows how to establish another profit center to offer other
publishers' books to your customers. Combining
complementary (non-competing) books with your books
makes your brochures and mailings more economical
while establishing you as a one-stop source for
information on your subject. This Report tells you how to
find complementary books, how to negotiate with their

publisher (even the big ones will give you 45% or more off if you approach the right department), and how to promote your new bookshelf. Includes an action plan and sample letters, and resources.
Document 632, 9 pages. See http://parapublishing.com/sites/para/information/fulfillme nt.cfm and scroll down.

COLD CALLING IS A BUSINESS SKILL THAT TERRIFIES MOST PEOPLE, yet it is an extraordinary tool for promoting oneself and one's books! See www.wendyweiss.com. Sign up for free prospecting and sales tips from Wendy Weiss, 'The Queen of Cold Calling." wendy@wendyweiss.com.

HOW TO SELL MORE BOOKS. Want to sell a lot more books? If your books aren't disappearing off the shelves bringing you the profits you deserve, you may want to learn about the top three things to take your book sales over the top. See *Three Things Each Author Needs to Sell Books* by Judy Cullins.
http://www.bookcoaching.com/freearticles.shtml

## SENIORS, BOOKS FOR

SENIOR MARKET ADVISOR is the only magazine written and edited specifically for agents, advisors, and planners who work directly with the 50+ market. Published monthly, it provides in-depth coverage on the issues and topics today's advisors face. See http://www.seniormarketadvisor.com.

## SHIPPING RATES & RESOURCES

AUTOMATE YOUR SHIPPING with free programs from UPS and FedEx. For UPS, call: (800) 742-5877. Ask for online Worldship information. For FedEx, call: (877) 339-2774. Ask for Ship Manager software.

COMPARE SHIPPING RATES, see information at http://www.intershipper.net.

SHIPPING RATES
--Domestic
USPS: http://postcalc.usps.gov
Books, CDs, cassettes, DVDs, and videos should all be marked "Media Mail" to secure the proper USPS rate.
UPS:
 http://wwwapps.ups.com/QCCWebApp/request

--International
USPS: http://ircalc.usps.gov
UPS: http://ups.com/using/services/rave/rate.html
FedEx: http://www.fedex.com/us/international

DROP-OFF LOCATIONS: Find out where to ship or arrange pickup.
USPS:
http://www.usps.com/pickup/welcome.htm?from=global&page=schedulepickup
UPS:
http://www.ups.com/using/services/locate/locate.html

FEDEX FOR LESS. FedEx Express Saver® gets delivered in about 3 days for as little as $7.95. See http://www.fedex.com/us/services/us/expresssaver.html. Thanks for this tip from Markus Allen.
http://www.markusallen.com

PRIORITY MAIL DELIVERIES CAN NOW BE TRACED with the USPS Delivery Confirmation™ service. Just purchase the bar-coded sticker for $.35 each.

TRACK YOUR PRIORITY MAIL AND PARCEL POST PACKAGES. See
http://www.framed.usps.com/cttgate/welcome.htm

TRACK YOUR UPS PACKAGES with your cell phone or PDA, see
http://www.ups.com/wireless. Ever ship packages to yourself at a hotel only to find they "haven't arrived"? Now you can whip out your cell phone or palm device to get the tracking information.

WHEN SHIPPING POSTAL M-BAGS TO OTHER COUNTRIES, stick the little green PS Form 2976 on the carton for the foreign Customs people. But, detach the white part and paperclip it to the PS Tag 158 for your Post Office. Otherwise, the postal employees have to open the sack to get the tag. And remember, the postage is totaled on the weight of the carton only not on the bag.

## SHREDDERS, PAPER

RECYCLE OFFICE WASTE. Use a paper shredder to turn waste paper into packing material.
--Ellen Searby, author of *The Costa Rica Traveler.*

## SOFTWARE

CONVERT FILES INTO ADOBE PDF. Try it for FREE.
https://createpdf.adobe.com

FREE DOWNLOADS OF GREAT SOFTWARE. Bookmark this site. See http://download.cnet.com.

## SPAM

AVOIDING SPAM & OTHER INTERNET INTRUSIONS. To protect your privacy and prohibit sites from collecting

data about your Internet browsing and buying habits, see the following sites: http://www.NetworkAdvertising.org and
http://www.AndersenCompliance.com.

**WANT TO REDUCE SPAM?** The Direct Marketing Association has launched E-MPS. Like their Mail Preference Service, you may place your name on their opt-out list indicating that you do not wish to receive email solicitations. DMA members are supposed to use this list to suppress e-MPS consumers from their own lists. See http://www.e-mps.org.

You can also fill in the opt-out form at the Direct Marketing Association. http://www.dm1.com. (That is a "one," not an "l."
--Linda Radke.

**WORDS NOT TO USE IN YOUR EMAIL MESSAGES.** Anti-spam controls used by some service providers will block messages with certain words. For a list, see Marcus Allen's website:
http://www.markusallen.org

**YOUR CUSTOMERS ARE YOUR COMPANY'S MOST VALUABLE ASSET.** Protect them from SPAM and other annoying intrusions while retaining their addresses for your own use. Treat their email address as you do their credit card numbers; never provide their contact information to anyone.

**SPEAKING, PROFESSIONAL**

Authors are expected to speak about their books. You can also get paid to speak.

Turning your books into speeches. Audiences want to hear from experts and the expert is the author of the book.

As Joe Vitale says: "The word authority has the word author in it."

Here are some speaking resources:

--Statistics on the professional speaking and meeting industries.
http://parapub.com/sites/para/resources/speakstats.cfm

--Harvey Mackay-35 Ways to Stay Alive. In the course of speaking to innumerable audiences all over the world, Mackay has gleaned invaluable tips and tricks for giving speeches in any setting. He shares them here in his "35 To Stay Alive."
http://www.mackay.com/howhelp/35alive.html

--SpeakerNet News ezine.
http://speakernetnews.com/subscribe.html

--Speak & Grow Rich, Dottie Walters.
http://www.speakandgrowrich.com/index.htm

--Speaking Coaching by Patricia Fripp.
http://www.fripp.com/

--Media Coaching by Joel Roberts.
JDRob36@aol.com

--Dan Poynter's speaking site. Example of an online media kit, etc.
http://parapub.com/sites/para/speaking/speechdesc.cfm

--Tom Antion's Speaking Resources
http://www.antion.com/

--Free reports on public speaking skills. See
http://www.schrift.com/tips.htm

--Sandra Schrift's Speaking FAQs.
http://www.schrift.com/executive/faqs.htm

--BarksBlog. Tips on speaking and the media industry by
Ed Barks
eBarks@BarksComm.comm   540-955-0600

--National Speakers Association, U.S..
http://www.NSAspeaker.org

--Toastmasters International
http://www.toastmasters.org

--Guide to Public Speaking and Speechwriting. . See
http://www.speechtips.com.

## STATISTICS

BOOK INDUSTRY STATISTICS.
=> Sales:
http://www.bookwire.com/bookwire/book_pub_industry_sa
les.htm
=> Reviews:
http://www.bookwire.com/bookwire/review_media_stats.h
tml
=> eBooks:
http://www.bookwire.com/bookwire/e-book_stats.htm

STATISTICS every writer should know:
http://www.nilesonline.com/stats

STATISTICS ON BOOK WRITING AND PUBLISHING.
There's a lot of valuable information of this fascinating

section        of        our        site.        See
http://parapub.com/sites/para/resources/statistics.cfm

PUBLISHING NUMBERS INCREASE DUE TO SELF-PUBLISHING AND POD PRINTING. The number of new book titles jumped from about 50,000 titles in 1985 to about 200,000 titles in 2004. The number of publishers jumped to more than 78,000 from well under half that in 1985 according to Frank J. Romano. See
http://www.ondemandjournal.com/dpc/dpc40.cfm
For more statistics, see
http://parapub.com/sites/para/resources/statistics.cfm
STATISTICAL CHALLENGE. 80% of U.S. families did not buy or read a book last year. 70% of U.S. adults have not been in a bookstore in the last five years. 58% of the adult U.S. population never reads another book after high school. Adults in the U.S. spent $5.4 billion on movies last year but they spent $25.6 billion on books. The pessimist says our market is smaller than we thought. The optimist says, our potential market is larger than we thought.

TV SETS ARE IN THE BEDROOMS of 50% of the kids in the U.S. aged 10-16.

## SUBMISSIONS

GUIDELINES FOR SUBMITTING BOOKS. To approach a publisher or agent, you must draft a book proposal. For detailed instructions,
see http://www.addicusbooks.com/submit.html

# T

## TAXES

IF YOU RECEIVE ROYALTIES FOR FOREIGN RIGHTS, get Form 6166 from the IRS to avoid (most) foreign taxes. Many other countries have tax treaties with the U.S. Foreign publishers and have to validate that you are paying taxes in the U.S. or they must withhold taxes for their own country. Refer to http://www.irs.gov to obtain the form online.
For questions, contact (215) 516-2000.

INDEPENDENT CONTRACTOR REPORTING. The State of California requires businesses to report the names and addresses of any independent contractor whose contract (verbal or written) exceeds or is likely to exceed $600 per year.

The stated purpose of the law is to allow the state to locate parents who are delinquent in their child-support obligations. The fact that you may not have children is irrelevant. The fact that you may not live in California is irrelevant.

This new requirement is not like 1099 reporting to the IRS because businesses must report names of independent contractors with whom they do business within 20 days of entering into a contract or making payments.

Peter Goodman has drafted an explanatory letter that may be sent to independent contractors. For a free copy, contact him at sbpedit@stonebridge.com

ROYALTIES (Form 1099-MISC) can now be reported to the IRS online. See http://www.irs.gov.

THE *SMALL BUSINESS RESOURCE GUIDE* CD-ROM 2005 from the U.S. Internal Revenue Service contains the tax forms, instructions, and publications needed by small business people. Included are checklists, tax data, and a business-plan form. It is available as Catalog Number 26757M free from the Internal Revenue Service at http://www.irs.gov. Tel: (800) 829-3676.

## TELEPHONE

ANSWERING THE TELEPHONE. Try a positive, helpful approach. Our example is as follows:
"Para Publishing, this is Dan Poynter and I *can* help you."

CALLER ID calls can be blocked to regular numbers. But calls to 800 numbers cannot be blocked because the *receiver* is paying for the call. Only the party paying for the call can block it. Also, Caller ID has nothing to do with unpublished numbers, even the unlisted numbers are revealed in Caller ID. You can obtain a readout from Radio Shack, and the service from the telephone company is inexpensive. In some states you get only the number a party is calling from but in others, you get the name, too. This is useful information for publishers who take telephone orders.

YOU MAY NOT WANT TO USE CALLER ID to greet callers by their names. When American Express used Caller ID technology to identify and greet incoming callers by name, they received numerous (privacy-related) complaints. It may be better to just answer with your company name and your name.

IF YOUR LONG-DISTANCE TELEPHONE RATES are not under $.05/minute, it is time to call your carrier and ask the magic question: "Do you have any new product?" All carriers are lowering rates and they are not telling present customers. When you call and use these words, they know you are rate shopping and they do not want to lose you. This works for cell service, too. We just cut our bill in half. The future? Look for monthly flat rate charges instead of per-minute charges.

ISO LIST OF COUNTRY CODES, view and print out: http:www.nw.com/zone/iso-country-codes.

PHONE SCAMS. People call saying they represent your telephone company. They may ask you to press 9-0-# to help them test your line. It really allows them to charge calls to your phone. Often the caller is in prison.

TELEPHONE AREA CODE LISTS, maps and proposed changes. Print out the latest to see current codes at http://www.nanpa.com.

TO GET AREA CODES, type in city/state at: http://www.555-1212.com/geo.isp

TELEPHONE NUMBERS. Clients are more likely to call if your number is easy to remember. The mnemonic is especially valuable when it relates to who you are or what you do. In order to find a telephone number that spells a recognizable word, see:
http://www.phonespelling.com/cgi-bin/result.cgi
http://www.PhoneSpell.org
http://www.dialABC.com
http://www.phonetic.com

AVOIDING TELEPHONE MENU TREES. Here is a company list that tells you in advance which buttons to push to get through to a human voice. See http://www.paulenglish.com/ivr/
--Godfrey Harris, www.harrisragan.com

Here at Para Publishing, we were lucky enough to get 800-PARAPUB that matches our URL: http://ParaPub.com. (Our main incoming line, 968-7277 also spells two common words starting with "Your". You will have to figure out the rest).

Once you locate some numbers you like, find out if they are available—just call them and hope for a telephone company recording.

WHEN SELECTING A TOLL-FREE NUMBER, call the 800, 888, and 877 variations. People will mix them up and call the wrong one. You do not want to pay for misdials. Try to avoid matching (high volume) catalog and customer service numbers.

TOLL-FREE NUMBER LOOKUP. Want a vanity number such as 800-PARAPUB? See https://small.bus.att.com/small_business/services/toll_free/lookup.jhtml.

TELEPHONE ORDER SHEET. Print out and keep several near each telephone. See Document 147 (free) at http://parapub.com/sites/para/resources/allproducts.cfm

## TITLES, BOOK

CINDY CASHMAN MADE A BUNDLE on *Everything Men Know About Women*. She sold more than 800,000 copies before selling out to Andrews and McMeel. The pages are blank. That demonstrates the importance of a title. (Just think how small her "print" bill was.)

Other blank books have been *The Snakes of Hawaii, Memoirs of an Amnesiac* and *The Nothing Book.* Cindy, you should be aware that the publisher of the Memoir book sued the publisher of the Nothing book for plagiarism. Not to worry, though, the Court held that "Nothingness" is in the public domain. cindy@CindyCashman.com

IF YOUR TITLE IS NOT SELLING THE BOOK, CHANGE IT. You can make any changes you wish in your next edition (the authority is confirmed to you by the First Amendment of the Constitution of the United States.) For a list of well-known books that had alternative original titles, see Document 156 at http://parapub.com/sites/para/resources/allproducts.cfm

NEED A THOUGHT STIMULATOR FOR PICKING A TITLE? See http://www.namingnewsletter.com.

SELECTING A BOOK TITLE THAT SELLS. Creating the title/sub-title will be the single-most important piece of copy writing you will do for that book. Your title/sub-title must be a selling tool. It is the hook that helps determine sales. Learn the basic elements of a catchy title and the never-to-be broken rules. Fascinating. Document 630, 7 pages. Scroll down at http://parapub.com/sites/para/resources/allproducts.cfm

TITLES SELL THE BOOK. Some six out of ten books on the bestseller lists have dynamite titles.

If your title is not selling the book, change it. You can make any changes you wish in your next edition (the authority is confirmed to you by the First Amendment of the Constitution of the United States.) See Document 156: book titles that were changed at http://parapub.com/sites/para/resources/allproducts.cfm

GET THE URL. When picking a title for your book, try to get the URL for it. Then, if a web surfer types in your book title, your site will pop up. For my book, *The Older Cat*, I secured oldercat.com and theoldercat.com (and several others).

TEST YOUR BOOK TITLE. The Title to a book is the headline that gets the attention of the public. Marketing experts all agree that you must test your headline to increase its pulling power. You can test up to 10 headlines at a time and have the focus group vote on which ones they feel are more effectively written. http://www.headlines2go.com
and
http://parapub.com/sites/para/information/writing.cfm

TITLE CHANGES. You can make any changes you wish in your next edition (the authority is confirmed to you by the First Amendment of the Constitution of the United States.) For a list of well-known books that had alternative original titles, see Document 156 at http://parapub.com/sites/para/resources/allproducts.cfm

WHEN WRITING TITLES, DO YOU PUT THEM IN ITALICS? Use italics for the titles and subtitles of publications (i.e., books, pamphlets, magazines, newspapers). For titles of articles, movies, programs, etc., use quotation marks, not italics.

## TRADE SHOWS

TRADE SHOW TIPS Online. Free ezine on book fairs and other trade shows. Edited by Marlys K. Arnold, a trade show marketing and image consultant, the tips cover a variety of exhibiting issues, from pre-show marketing to booth staff behavior to following up on leads. Having also worked in author promotions for a local bookstore, Arnold has counseled numerous authors and publishers on how to make their books stand out from the hundreds of others on the shelf. To sign up, go to http://www.egroups.com/subscribe/tradeshowtips

## TRANSLATION

TO TRANSLATE TO AND FROM English, Spanish, French, German, Italian, Portuguese, and more see http://www.systransoft.com.

## TRAVEL BOOKS. RESOURCES

TRAVEL BOOKS. Resources for Writing, Producing and Promoting Guidebooks. Lists the information sources you need to successfully publish and promote travel books. Document 616, 5 pages. See http://parapub.com/sites/para/information/writing.cfm and scroll down.

TRAVEL PUBLICATIONS UPDATE lists nearly 600 magazines and 220 newspaper travel sections. The directory is on disk for $30. Fmi: Travel Marketing Sources, Tel: (510) 654-3035; email: PatSnide@aol.com

TRAVEL TO PLACES THAT HAVE A LITERARY CONNECTION. Also read about writers and creative artists and the places they have lived and traveled. See http://www.literarytraveler.com.
—Wally Bock

TRAVEL WRITING RESOURCES. See

http://www.transitionsabroad.com/listings/travel/travel_writing/index.shtml

## TRIM SIZE

WHAT SIZE AND FORMAT SHOULD YOUR BOOK BE? --Ron "Hobie" Hobart, Dunn+Associates Design, http://www.dunn-design.com

Hardcover or softcover? Dust jacket? French flaps? 5.5 x 8.5" or 6 x 9"? Your professional book cover designer will help you determine the best size for your book. And your distributor may have some valuable input for you regarding the appropriate format for your topic and audience.

In the bookstores there may be a current trend away from hardcover and toward softcover book within a particular genre. Gift books are usually smaller whereas technical books are often larger.

If your book has a journal or workbook feature, be sure to ask for lay-flat binding so it is easier to use. If you are printing digitally, you may find better price breaks at the 5.5 x 8.5" size vs the 6 x 9" size. Your designer will prefer the 6 x 9" size because it provides greater opportunity to cash in on that expanded valuable real estate. See http://www.BookCoverTips.com

## TYPESETTING

IDENTIFY A TYPEFACE. See http://www.identifont.com.

NEED SOMEONE TO DESIGN, TYPESET AND LAYOUT YOUR BOOK? See the Supplier List at http://parapub.com/sites/para/resources/supplier.cfm

SAN SERIF TYPEFACES: ARIAL V HELVETICA. See amaclaren@chuck-maclarenlaw.com
--Pete Masterson, http://www.aeonix.com

# U

## USED BOOKS

BISG STUDIES SALES OF USED BOOKS. See http://www.forewordmagazine.com/ftw/ftwarchives.aspx?id=20051005.htm

# V

## VERTICAL FILE

If you have a report priced at $12 or less, you may list it in H. W. Wilson's Vertical File Index. VFI is sent to libraries and a mention usually results in a number of sales. Send your report with full bibliographic information to H. W. Wilson Co., 950 University Ave., Bronx, New York 10452; (800) 367-6770. http://www.hwwilson.com/print/vfi.html.

## VIRAL MARKETING

"VIRAL MARKETING" is when you send out an email message to a few friends or associates and they forward it to others in their email address book. Those recipients forward it and so on. Now the group receiving your email is growing geometrically as your message affects (not "infects" ☺ ) an ever-increasing number of people.

Your viral missive may be humorous, a deeply moving story or a valuable piece of information that recipients feel compelled to share with others. If you have cleverly designed your message around your book or subject matter, the exposure to it will grow like a chain letter. The best part of this viral proliferation of your sales message is that it comes with an implied endorsement of the forwarder.

UNLEASHING THE IDEA VIRUS: Stop Marketing *at* People: Turn Your Ideas into Epidemics by Helping Your Customers do the marketing for you by Seth Godin. http://www.sethgokin.com/ideavirus

# W

**WEBSITES**

THE PARA PUBLISHING WEBSITE (ParaSite?) is a great place to learn about book promotion. There is a lot of editorial material on everything from writing through production, the business of books to promotion. The site lists resources such as 40 books, 39 short reports, and nine long reports. There is a list of suppliers to the industry, the newsletter archive, book promotion mailing lists, research links, a place to display your own book free (Success Stories), news announcements and a place to get a free information kit. See http://ParaPub.com

DO-IT-YOURSELF WEBSITES. Now authors and publishers can have an online presence without webmaster fees. See http://www.AmericanAuthor.com.

## FIVE QUESTION-FIVE MINUTE WEB MAKEOVER QUIZ
--Judy Cullins, 20-year bookcoach,
http://www.bookcoaching.com

If you haven't made Web sales and built your clients to an income you want, then maybe you need a Web Site makeover.

What I mean by that is, most people first contact a webmaster to put up their site. They can connect the links but not all are copywriters that bring in new customers and clients. You may have written your own material, but often it lacks the promotion know how to make your words sell. Take this quiz and the next step Web Marketing with stimulating sales copy writing.

Score the below questions from 0-5. Add up the total and see the recommendations at the end.

1. Does your home page include headlines that compel your visitor to click to product or service sales letter?

The number one mistake Web site owners make is not to give their valuable visitors a reason to buy. While mission statements and bios talk about you, benefit driven headlines make the difference--showing your potential buyers what outcomes they will receive.

2. Does your site offer a sales letter for each product or service you want to sell?

Visitors want you to help them make an informed decision. Educate them about your service in this piece whether it's in a long or short sales letter. If it's a product give them a reason to buy. Include benefits, features, and of course testimonials.

3. Do you make it easy for your visitor to buy?

At the end of your sales letter, include an order page on how to buy. Include each step because many people online are non-techie like your Internet marketing coach. Include the call the action link that takes your visitor straight to the order page. Check out a professional's site to see these skills in action.

4. Do you give your visitors what they want--f.ree information?

Not only does a list of articles, ezines or tips on your site give f.ree content--what visitors want--it also helps your site become number 1 to 10 in the search engines. That means 1000's of visitors a day. And that means more consistent monthly sales. Your non-techie Web coach is still number one in Google and 35 others after four years with the word "bookcoaching". Content is what makes people bookmark your site to return again and again.

5. Does your Web site bring you all the income you want?

Your site may be attractive and colorful, but check you monthly sales and make sure they increase to the income you want. It's not the hits, its the sales that really matter. Naturally, your site brings new contacts and develops an image too, but remember to measure your web site's success by the income it provides. Otherwise it's not worth a dime.

Recommendations

Score 0-4
If your score less than 5 you are ready for a complete makeover. Get help now.

Score 5 to 7
Your site is not doing much for your business. It needs improvement. Get a comprehensive Web site evaluation.

Score 8 to 10
Your site is doing well, but a web strategy could make it more successful.

Score greater than 10
Your Web site works. Get ongoing feedback for adding new content and making link changes. Realize your site cannot be static, and must keep growing and service your particular audience.

Putting up a Web site is not enough. It must give your targeted visitors what they want--free content, and it's copy must be punchy and persuasive to get your visitor to convert to a customer.

WANT A WEB SITE DESIGNED OR PROMOTED? See the Supplier List at
http://parapub.com/sites/para/resources/supplier.cfm

HOW THE RIGHT URL CAN HELP YOU SELL MORE BOOKS
--Susan Kendrick/Graham Van Dixhorn,
http://www.WriteToYourMarket.com

When you're trying to come up with a great title for your book, make sure to take this step. Go to a domain registration website, such as www.misk.com, and check for the availability of the title as a URL. This does two things. First, you find out if someone else already has a web presence under the name you are considering. Second, having this URL--preferably the .com--gives you an easy, memorable way to quickly point buyers to your book website in your online marketing; in print, radio, and TV interviews; and more. We've seen authors lose huge sales potential even after national TV exposure, simply because they gave out a long, obscure, or hard-to-remember website address. We've seen other authors rake in sale after sale with a book title and website address that make it easy for buyers to remember the name of the book--and where to buy it! For more ways to use URLs to your advantage and for proven strategies for coming up with just the right title for your book—plus a F.REE consultation to get you started or help you with the final decision...Go to www.CoverThatBook.com and click on "New Double CD." Request the special coupon code and save 20% instantly.

## WOMEN, BOOKS FOR

According to Markus Allen, the Journal of Financial Planning reports that 24% of women buy an item simply because it's on sale. And Lou Aronica, Senior VP Avon Books, says that women purchase 68% of the books.

WOMEN'S STUDIES BOOKS WANTED FOR REVIEW. Send to: Women's Studies, Resource and Research Center, George Mason University, Fairfax, VA 22030; Tel: (703) 993-2896.

## WRITERS, WRITING

BOOK WRITING TIPS & RESOURCES. See http://parapub.com/sites/para/information/writing.cfm.

FREELANCE WRITING ORGANIZATION provides all kinds of writing information for fiction, non-fiction, journalism, screenplays, plays, comedy, Internet, TV, radio, poetry and more, are available. Plus artist profiles, interviews, features and professional writing resources and links for editors, journalists and writers of all mediums. See http://www.fwointl.com/in.html.

HELP FOR WRITERS. See www.SimonTeakettle.com. —Barbara Florio Graham

INTROVERTS COMPRISE 25% OF THE U.S. POPULATION. Writers tend to be introverts. Most writers are reluctant to promote their books on radio, TV or in stores. Help is on the way. We won't try to change you; we will describe easy ways to promote your books without leaving home.

PAPERPOINT SEMINAR ON BOOK WRITING WITH DAN POYNTER. If you or a colleague is in the writing stage on a nonfiction book, get this freebie now. Listen at http://www.michaelport.com/audio/PF2_DanPoynter.mp3 and Get the handout at http://parapub.com/sites/para/speaking/formsbank.cfm. Scroll down and download the three pieces of P-47. Then look at the Template and slides and listen to the seminar. This PaperPoint seminar is just like being there.

INFOKITS. Detailed information on book writing, production, promotion and distribution. http://parapub.com/sites/para/resources/infokit.cfm

SEVEN SECRETS OF WRITING A BOOK THAT SELLS! So what are the secrets to writing a book that sells? Request our special report and we'll show you what it takes to not just write a great book but sell it as well! You can request this free report by sending an email to: penny@amarketingexpert.com?subject=sevensecrets —Penny C. Sansevieri

VALUABLE RESOURCES FOR WRITERS. See:

—AbsoluteWrite.com
http://www.AbsoluteWrite.com
—The Writer
http://www.writermag.com
—Worldwide Freelance Writer Newsletter
http://www.worldwidefreelance.com
—Writer's Digest
http://www.writersdigest.com
—WritersWeekly.com
http://www.writersweekly.com

(The librarians' resource. See http://lii.org.)

WHEN LEARNING A NEW BUSINESS OR TRADE, the apprentice always starts with the small jobs. For example: A beginner auto mechanic might start with an oil change, not overhauling a transmission. The same approach applies with book publishing. Learn your strengths and weaknesses after publishing two or three mini reads, such as a 1-page newsletter, a 10-page chapbook, or a 20-page eBook. Then you will be better equipped to publish your big project.
--Judine Slaughter, http://class.universalclass.com/diy101

WANT TO SUMMARIZE YOUR BOOK? In MS-Word, see Tools\AutoSummarize. You may condense your book to some 25% of its original size in a couple of minutes. — Dan Burrus

WRITE THAT BOOK: GET IT CLEAR, GET IT DOWN, GET IT OUT by Serena Williamson, Ph.D. This inspirational gem is perfect if you have a million ideas swimming around in your head and can't seem to get started. Serena gets you laser-focused with your perfect title and strategic plan. She eliminates barriers, and gets your book written, published and launched in record time. By the way, as a special bonus, when you buy her

book you get two free gifts …two gifts that can make you a best-seller. See
http://www.bookcoachpress.com/products/

140 ARTICLES ON BOOK WRITING, SELF AND ePUBLISHING, AND PROMOTION by Judy Cullins.
http://www.bookcoaching.com/freearticles.shtml

WRITING YOUR BOOK. Thinking/planning, writing and deciding on publishing: Get an agent, find a publisher or publish yourself.
http://parapub.com/sites/para/information/writing.cfm
PAPERPOINT SEMINAR ON BOOK WRITING WITH DAN POYNTER. If you or a colleague are in the writing stage on a nonfiction book, get this freebie now. Listen at
http://www.michaelport.com/audio/PF2_DanPoynter.mp3
and
Get the handout at
http://parapub.com/sites/para/speaking/formsbank.cfm
Scroll down and download the three pieces of P-47.
Then look at the Template and slides and listen to the seminar.
This PaperPoint seminar is just like being there.

# X, Y, Z.

# Colophon

**Research and gathering**
Most of the resources appeared in editions of *Publishing Poynters*

**Writing and manuscript building**
Manuscript preparation: MS-Word
Editing: Karen Stedman, Penmark
Typefaces:
> Body text: Century 11 pt.
> Headers: Arial 12 pt bold.
> Section heads: Century, 18 pt.
> Alphabet: Century 28 pt.
> Stories: Tahoma bold, 10 pt.

**Prepress**
Cover design by Robert Howard of RH Graphic Design.
rhoward@frii.com

**Conversion**
MS-Word to PDF: Adobe Acrobat 7.0

**Printing**
Printing of softcover book: LightningSource, POD.
Paper
> 5.5 x 8.5: Creme 55lb./ 85gsm
> 8.5 x 11 Large Print: White 50lb./ 75gsm
Cover: 10 pt C1S, four color, layflat film lamination.
Conversion of eBook: RosettaMachine.com
Distribution of eBook: RosettaMachine.com and LightningSource.com

# Index